CRIMES & MISDEEDS

Headlines from Arizona's Past

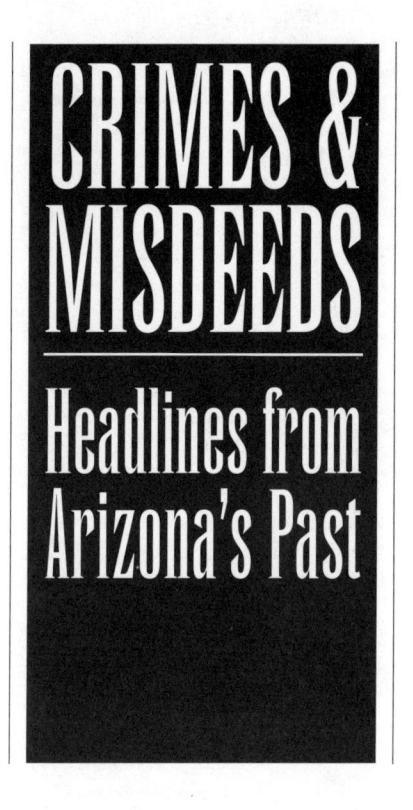

CRIMES & MISDEEDS

Headlines from Arizona's Past

W. Lane Rogers

NORTHLAND PUBLISHING

The display type was set in Runic Condensed.
The text type was set in Wessex.
Designed by Sandy Bell
Edited by Rodney Nelson and Stephanie Bucholz
Production supervised by Lisa Brownfield

Manufactured in the United States of America by Publishers Press

Photo credits: Arizona Historical Society/Central Arizona Division, page 55;
Arizona Historical Society/Tucson, pages 4 (B#28164), 5 (B#29274), 13 (#30458), 16,
44 (#46734), 45 (#1381), 59 (#60143), 70 (#17617), 94 (#12101), 97 (#1484),
98 (#12977), 100 (#54106), 101 (#28383), and 119 (#60762);
Utah State Historical Society, pages 124 and 127;
W. Lane Rogers, pages 34 and 35.

FIRST EDITION
ISBN 0-87358-631-x
Library of Congress Catalog Card Number 95-11110
Cataloging-in-Publication Data

Rogers, W. Lane, 1944-
Crimes and misdeeds : headlines from Arizona's past / W. Lane Rogers. – 1st ed.
p. cm.
Includes bibliography references and index.
ISBN 0-87358-631-X (pbk.)
1. Crime–Arizona–History. 2. Criminals–Arizona–History. I. Title.
HV6793.A6R65 1995   95-11110
364.9791–dc20

COVER:
*John Dillinger photographed by the Tucson Police Department,
courtesy of the Arizona Historical Society/Tucson.*

0562/5M/8-95

THIS BOOK
IS LOVINGLY DEDICATED
TO DOROTHY N. ROGERS.
ALWAYS DID SHE KEEP
THE FAITH.

Contents

Acknowledgments

The author is indebted to the late Whitney Stine, whose books were an inspiration—his encouragement and advice over many years, invaluable. To Wallace E. Clayton, a wordsmith of no small repute, is owed a debt of gratitude for his keen and sensitive eye, for his intransigent insistence on getting it right. Countless hours were spent in the libraries of the Arizona Historical Society and the University of Arizona. Gratitude is expressed to the many professionals who aided in my research. Thanks are due Kate Riley who, during the last phase of preparation, generously assisted in polishing the manuscript. And, of course, a loving thank you to my wife, Patricia, who claims—quite erroneously—never to interrupt me when I am writing. She contributed considerable research to this volume, and, as composer Richard Strauss' wife was wont to say during his idle moments, she often would say to me, Rogers, "go write something."

Chapter 1

The Dillinger Gang in Tucson

DURING THE PREDAWN HOURS of January 21, 1934, a defective furnace in the basement of the Hotel Congress ignited woodwork dry with age. Flames leaped at the structure's walls, and soon one of Tucson's finest hostelries was engulfed by fire. Firemen, responding to the alarm, swept through the building, banging on the doors of its sleeping guests. People in various states of dress and undress were evacuated from their rooms and ushered outside into the early morning chill. Oddly enough, a resident of the top floor seemed more concerned about his luggage than himself and gave firefighters a fuss when ordered to leave the building. His agitation continued as he strode outside the hotel and watched flames shoot skyward, and his histrionics proved successful. Two firemen were persuaded to reenter the burning building and retrieve several heavy, expensive-looking bags from his room.

Drawn to the scene by billowing smoke, Tom Duck, an undergraduate at the University of Arizona, watched as firemen hauled luggage down from the third floor on ropes. Pitching in, the young man carried several bags to the safety of a nearby grass island.

More than fifty years later, Duck would recall a well-dressed man approaching him from behind. "Hey, kid, will you watch my luggage for me?" the stranger had asked, flaunting a ten-dollar bill.

"Ten dollars was a heck of a lot of money in those days," recounted Duck, noting that the nation was in the midst of the worst depression in its history. "It would be like someone today offering a hundred dollars to have their bags looked after. It made me real uneasy."

Three days after the blaze, the firemen who had rescued the bags glanced at a photo in "The Lineup" section of *True Detective Mysteries*, a popular magazine of the day. They were struck by its resemblance to the man who had protested so loudly about his luggage.

The face in the photo belonged to Russell Clark. No run-of-the-mill criminal, Clark was a member of the notorious John Dillinger gang and was wanted for murder and bank robbery. He had registered at the Congress under the alias Arthur Long, claiming to be a Florida tourist.

The same man had given pause to a couple of vacationing New Yorkers who crossed paths with him at a local nightclub the previous evening. In the company of two men and three women, the man was heard to boast how easy it was to earn a livelihood robbing banks. The startled vacationers paid close attention, noting that each of the men was armed. Later, they reported their discovery to the police department.

After checking identification records, it was established that the men in the armed trio were not well-heeled Florida tourists but the infamous criminals, Russell Clark, "Fat" Charlie Makley, and Harry Pierpont, each traveling with a female companion—all members of "Bad" John Dillinger's murderous gang. Dillinger himself had not been seen, but police surmised he was not far away.

All at once, a small police force in a dusty desert town was faced with the task of apprehending America's most-wanted gangsters. It was a chilling notion. The men they sought were cold-blooded killers who would not quibble about unloading their weapons into the bellies of Tucson's finest. Pierpont, known to be mentally unbalanced, presented the greatest risk. He was a man who killed for pleasure.

"Fat" Charlie Makley proved easy to capture. Spotted in a radio-repair shop on Congress Street, he was asked to come to the police station for a routine check of his automobile's papers. Confident they were in order, he went along with no resistance. Once inside the station, the officers fingerprinted and positively identified Makley as the hoodlum he was.

Russell Clark was not a willing captive. Traced to a rented house on North Second Avenue near the university, he was found with his girlfriend, Opal Love, a busty redhead nicknamed "the Mack Truck." Clark put up a fight that left him with a split scalp. A search of the premises revealed the expensive-looking bags firemen had rescued and Duck had guarded.

In them was an assortment of machine guns, pistols, ammunition and bullet-proof vests.

Harry Pierpont was discovered driving along South Sixth Avenue in the Armory Park neighborhood. Two officers pulled him over near Nineteenth Street and, using the same tactic they had used to collar Makley, asked that he accompany them to the police station for a check of the paperwork on his out-of-state auto. He agreed and an officer rode with him in the backseat, his unholstered gun concealed between jittery legs. Once inside the station, Pierpont noticed the gang's arsenal and began to put up a fight, but he was overpowered by several officers who stripped him of his weapons—including a pistol dangling down his back on a piece of string.

With these three lieutenants in custody, the search now focused on the elusive Dillinger. Confident he would show up at the rented house on North Second Avenue, the dwelling was placed under constant surveillance. What no one knew was that Dillinger had registered under an assumed name at the Close-Inn Tourist Court on South Sixth Avenue in South Tucson, not far from the spot where Pierpont had been picked up. Had he not paid a visit to his cohorts, he might never have been apprehended—at least not in Tucson.

He had registered under the name Frank Sullivan, octogenarian Eugene Glass remembered a half century later. Glass, who was twenty-seven years old at the time, did not recall meeting the gangster but knew bartenders at the Shamrock who did.

Built in 1927 by Glass' father, Jester, the Close-Inn was a complex of more than forty tourist bungalows sprawling a block long on South Sixth Avenue with an annex across the street. The Shamrock Bar anchored the family business at the south end, and Dillinger was a frequent patron during his Tucson sojourn. No one knew his real identity, but the barkeeps found it curious that he always sat in a booth near the back door. "If someone else was sitting at the booth, Dillinger would pay the bartender to get them to move," recalled Glass. "[I] guess he wanted to be by that backdoor in case he had to get out of there in a hurry."

On the evening of January 25 Dillinger and his traveling companion, Evelyn Frechette, parked his newly acquired brown Hudson in front of the North Second Avenue bungalow and started up the walk. Three police officers sprang into action. According to the *Tucson Citizen*, one officer said, "Stick 'em up!" while another said, "Reach for the moon or I'll cut you in two!"

Caught completely off guard by the stakeout, Dillinger was arrested without incident. His only words were, "Well, I'll be damned!"

With nary a shot fired, America's Public Enemy Number One and three of his subordinates were behind bars. With breathless speed, newspaper headlines and radio commentators spread the news around the globe. Within hours, the eyes of the world focused on the Pima County jail, and Tucson was bathed in a blinding light of publicity.

With self-deprecating humor and biting sarcasm, the *Arizona Daily Star* editorialized that "scoffing at hick town cops is never good business. It wasn't good business for the Dillingers, at any rate. They were so cocksure of the hicktownishness of Tucson that they didn't hesitate to patronize the roadhouses and cabarets, singly and together, and display rolls of money, handing out one-hundred-dollar bills here, five-hundred-dollar bills there, and generally making themselves as conspicuous as it was possible to do. They might have known that this is bad business in a big city and still worse business in a small one.

"The hick town police didn't know anything about policing. You see, they had not learned under the Al Capone influence in Chicago or other

North Second Avenue bungalow where Dillinger was captured.

Pierpont, Makley, and Dillinger photographed by the Tucson Police Department.

Midwest centers. They had an idea that a gangster was a bad citizen and should be arrested....

"All of which is by way of saying that John Dillinger and his gang made a terrible mistake when they tried to use Tucson as a hideout."

While law-enforcement officials in larger cities and states that had been unable to capture Dillinger and his men, or keep them behind bars, looked with bemusement at Tucson, the nation's top G-man—who had had precious little luck himself—paid his compliments. According to a January 26 Associated Press (AP) dispatch, "J. Edgar Hoover, chief of the Federal Department of Justice, today expressed ... his satisfaction with the performance of Tucson and county peace officers in effecting the capture of the Dillinger gang." An understatement at best.

The gangster himself, a man not known for reticence, had a good deal to say and told his captors, "You were awfully lucky. When you were smart was getting one of us at a time. If you had gone in that house when Clark and Makley were both there, it would have been too bad. There were guns in the back room. It would have been a fight. Some of us might have been shot, but some of you would have been shot too."

Local residents buzzed with speculation about the gang's motives. Had they come to Tucson to hide out or to pull a job? Because "Fat" Charlie Makley had been seen in a downtown shop examining police radios, many people thought the latter was the more likely scenario. If indeed the examination of police radios had been a prelude to pulling a job, then the gang failed to do its homework. In 1934 the Tucson Police Department, like many of its counterparts nationwide, had yet to join the electronic age and was without radio equipment of any kind.

Harry Pierpont, the most ruthless of Dillinger's henchmen, said, as reported by AP, "We came here to get away from the bad weather." He was not, however, making reference to climate. "Tucson is a cold town," he added with a play on words, "and back east all the towns are hot."

Some two thousand men, women, and children gathered about the Pima County Courthouse, hoping to glimpse the infamous Dillinger's face as the badman was led to his arraignment. Constant F. Weinzapfel was one of the spectators. "It seemed like the whole town was there," he recalled more than half a century later. "Fox Movietone came over from Los Angeles and filmed the thing. Later I found out that my face had been on movie screens all over the country."

Guards armed with machine guns, rifles, pistols, and tear gas maintained an all-night vigil, and in the morning, the entire courthouse was cordoned off. One officer was given the task of checking the identity of passengers in out-of-state cars parked near the courthouse; another was stationed on the stairs leading to the jail; a third was placed near the door from which the prisoners entered the corridor leading to superior court. All entrances to the sheriff's office were under heavy guard, and no one was permitted entry until his identity and official status were verified.

Bail was set at $100,000 for each man, an extremely large sum of money until one considers that Dillinger was arrested with some $6,000 in his pocket and more than $40,000 was found among the gang members and their female companions.

While authorities in Indiana, Ohio, and Wisconsin argued heatedly that each had extradition rights to the quartet of fugitives, nervous Tucson lawmen feared that one of the gang leader's mob would post bail and set one or all free, or worse, set them free by storming the jail with machine guns—not a farfetched notion. Anxious over the possibility of bloodshed and their possible inability to control it, Arizona officials wanted Dillinger and his men out of the state—fast.

At last, a deal was struck, and Dillinger's home state of Indiana was awarded the spoils. Wanted there for murder, bank robbery, and a variety of lesser charges, Dillinger would have been perfectly content to remain in Tucson, where his treatment was tantamount to that of a celebrity. Because he refused jailhouse food, his meals were catered by a nearby restaurant, and to ease boredom, his Boston terrier puppy was brought to his cell for amusement.

When told he would be extradited to Indiana the same afternoon, Dillinger threw a tantrum and, according to the *Arizona Daily Star*, fought like a "wildcat" when officials attempted to manacle his wrists. He was subdued against the wall of his cell, and his hands were cuffed behind his back and his legs shackled securely. The gangster was then spirited away to the Tucson airport, put aboard a monoplane, and flown southeast to the Mexican border town of Douglas, where he was incarcerated in the city jail for a night of safekeeping.

There he was met by Police Chief Percy Bowden, who escorted Dillinger to a cell, removed his cuffs and shackles, and told the prisoner that he would make things as comfortable for him as possible but he was not to pull anything. "At this," writes Ervin Bond, Bowden's biographer, "Dillinger said that the thing he wanted most was a good night's sleep." A guard was posted outside the cell, and extra men were placed about the exterior of the building.

The night passed uneventfully, and the next morning, Dillinger asked if he could shave before leaving on the next leg of the trip to Indiana. The police chief "fixed him a safety razor, and he and the guard watched him very closely as he shaved.... They had some fear that he might try to commit suicide.

"About thirty minutes before they were to take him to the airport east of town," continues Bond, "Percy had him brought to his office with only handcuffs on." Reportedly, the two had a conversation in which Dillinger said that he was not so bad as the FBI made him out to be, that he had never killed anyone.

When asked why he had gone to Tucson rather than flee into Mexico, the captured fugitive said that "he did not speak Spanish, and he had heard about their jails and dungeons and never did want to get into one. He also said that two of his men . . . had paid a visit to Douglas after they heard about the large smelter payrolls, and cased the two banks across the street from each other. They stopped overnight and stayed close to the police station in the Palomar Hotel. They even played some card games with a few local people. They checked around and, when they returned to Tucson, reported to Dillinger that if they pulled the job, there was no way out except south into Mexico. . . . [Dillinger] decided to call that scheme off."

In a tale that rings apocryphal, the prisoner is said to have given Bowden a twenty-dollar Canadian gold piece as a measure of his appreciation for the police chief's kindness. Given that Dillinger was considered one of the most dangerous men in America, the likelihood of Tucson authorities' allowing the criminal to carry money in his pocket is improbable at best.

A tale that rings with authenticity, however, is Bond's assertion that Bowden was told by Dillinger "that there wasn't a jail in the United States that he could not break out of."

Soon Dillinger was aboard an American Airways plane. While the first airline hijacking would be far in the future, no chances were taken, and he was shackled to the steel brace supporting the pilot's seat—in the custody of the Crown Point, Indiana, sheriff.

"He was well behaved throughout the trip and hardly said a word," commented one of the guards. "Apparently, he is resigned to his fate."

The largest police escort ever assembled in Chicago was on hand when the badman's plane landed at the airport. With more than one hundred officers guarding his arrival, the chained criminal was taken to a heavily armed motorcade of twenty vehicles, which would deliver him across the state line to the Lake County jail.

"Every light . . . gleamed as Dillinger took the few steps from his automobile to the inside of the jail," wrote the Associated Press upon the gangster's arrival in Indiana. "Armed deputies swarmed about the car and deputies even stood atop the jail as the prisoner, handcuffed . . . climbed out . . . [of the vehicle].

"Reports that some of the gangster['s] friends, who once liberated him from an Ohio jail after killing a sheriff, were on their way to attempt a delivery failed to materialize.

"Mrs. Lillian Holley, sheriff, typically feminine in appearance, without a weapon on her, expressed every confidence she would be able to keep the prisoner safe until after the trial."

In yet another AP story, Sheriff Holley told the reporter, "I think a lot of these stories about Dillinger are somewhat exaggerated.

"Just the same, though, we'll have a few extra guards in the jail while he is there and they'll be on the job with machine guns, too." She went on to say that Dillinger's solitary cell would be "constantly under the eyes of an armed guard patrolling the iron-barred hall leading to it. You know, we've never had a jail [break] here."

But as Holley would discover all too soon, there are few absolutes in life.

Thirty-one days after his arrival at Crown Point, Indiana, Dillinger, armed with a machine gun, walked out of the "escape-proof" Lake County jail to disappear into the bowels of the Midwest and resume his reign of terror.

No sooner had the gangster taken his leave from Mrs. Holley's institution than sightings were reported from one corner of the United States to another. "John Dillinger has been seen two hundred times in one day— sometimes in ten places at the same time," wrote the *Chicago Tribune*. In Tucson, the license number of a Ford coupé was broadcast over the radio after sightings in Brawley and San Bernardino, California and over the Arizona border at Yuma. According to the *Tribune*, "Chief C. A. Wollard of the Tucson police believes that his department can take care of itself if bandits decide to enter the city again."

In Agua Prieta, Sonora, Douglas' Mexican neighbor, the *Arizona Daily Star* reported that "Half a dozen reputable citizens and fully a dozen dancing girls in night clubs firmly assert the notorious American outlaw spent a night—and about one thousand dollars—at one of the night clubs. . . ."

And so it went until July 22, 1934, when Dillinger was met by Melvin H. Purvis and sixteen of his assistants. "John Dillinger, America's Public Enemy No. 1 and the most notorious criminal of recent time," reported the *Los Angeles Times*, "was shot and killed at 10:40 o'clock tonight by Federal agents a few seconds after he had left the Biograph Theatre, a neighborhood motion picture house on Chicago's North Side."

In February 1935, the Hudson driven by Dillinger to the house on North Second Avenue was sold at auction to a Tucsonan for $655. Rings, watches, and other personal items of gang members were auctioned off at the Pima County Courthouse. Some two hundred people shelled out $448 for hoodlum souvenirs. Even the police department got its piece of the spoils.

"Guns taken from the Dillinger gang in Tucson are, at long last, about to be turned over to the Tucson police department where they belong," editorialized the *Arizona Daily Star*. "With this new armament, officers of the department will at last have something with which to protect themselves effectively when and if they are called upon to meet similar desperate gangs in the future."

A few months later, Edward G. Robinson, "the hard-boiled principal of many a Hollywood gangster film," made a one-day visit to Tucson and "showered police officers with questions about the capture," according to the *Tucson Citizen*. And from that day forward, Hollywood would be the principal disseminator of information–or misinformation–about the life and times of John Dillinger. Rarely, if ever, would his Tucson capture figure in the telling.

Chapter 2

Eva: The Only Woman Executed in Arizona

ABOVE THE CONDEMNED CELLS on the second floor of the Arizona State Prison at Florence was a small, drab room. Because of its singular purpose, the room was not often used. Death was its sole function, the scaffold its only machinery. Directly below, separated by a trap door, was a second room. Into it would fall bodies dangling from rope's-end, breathing their last breaths. On its walls in glass cases were photographs of sixteen persons—all men—who had died there. Each was framed by the noose that had ended his life. Many Arizonans hoped a seventeenth photograph would be added—one that would offer a striking departure.

She had been born Eva McDaniels at Salisbury, Missouri, in 1878. Her fifth husband gave her the name Dugan, and that is the name she would take to a pauper's grave on the prison grounds at Florence.

Eva's odyssey began during the early days of January 1927, when she went to work as a housekeeper for Andrew J. Mathis. A recluse, Mathis was owner of a small chicken ranch on North Oracle Road at the outskirts of Tucson, Arizona. For reasons that remain obscure, Eva was fired after a couple of weeks. Rumor claimed she had tried to poison his meals. Mathis told neighbors he had driven her from his ranch and ordered her never to return. But Eva did return and with a vengeance.

Sometime around January 19, 1927, Mathis disappeared. With him disappeared his nearly new Dodge coupé, recently paid off, and other personal possessions. What no one knew is that Mathis—fifty-eight years old, slight of build, and in poor health—had been bludgeoned to death and bore a three-inch gash on the left side of his skull. A shallow grave had been dug on an obscure patch of his ranch land, and into it went the corpse. Before the first shovelful of dirt had been sprinkled over the body, chloride of lime was added to the grave to hasten decomposition. It did its job.

But Eva had made a mistake. Before fleeing in the Dodge, she offered neighbors an opportunity to purchase some of the dead man's belongings. Mathis had given them to her, then gone off to California, she said. It was an unlikely story. The rancher was not known for his generosity, and neighbors knew he had no use for the woman. Eva became a suspect in a supposed murder. But there was no body. Soon there was no Eva.

Later, she would claim that an itinerant ranch hand named Jack, who, it was said, had worked on the Mathis spread two days, bludgeoned the owner to death and forced Eva to accompany him in the stolen auto. It was an interesting tale, but one that did not wash well. Fact was that Eva and Jack—if that was his name—had driven the Dodge to Amarillo, Texas where the car was sold for six hundred dollars. Eva represented herself as Mrs. Eva Mathis and introduced Jack as A. J. Mathis, her son. She then forged a signature on the title and collected the money. Jack was never heard from again.

More than one hundred volunteers scoured the Mathis ranch in search of a body. They scanned the brush, cacti, and arroyos but found nothing. Officers, however, did find a charred ear trumpet (Mathis had been nearly deaf) in the ashes of an old wood stove. That discovery intensified the assumption that the chicken rancher had met with a violent demise.

A two-hundred-dollar reward was offered for Eva, one hundred dollars for information about Mathis. The task of finding the woman fell to Pima County Sheriff Jim McDonald. Eva's movements were traced from Texas to Chicago, to Buffalo, New York, to New York City. At last, Eva was found working in a hospital at White Plains, New York. McDonald, accompanied by the county attorney, pleaded his case before authorities at the capitol in Albany, and extradition papers were signed.

On March 4, 1927, the Apache Limited made a special stop at Vail station in Arizona to unload McDonald and his prisoner. They motored the remaining distance to Tucson, where Eva was charged in the theft of the Mathis automobile. Because no body had been found, murder charges could not be lodged.

Eva's stout, matronly form became a fixture in the Arizona press. Had color photography been available, readers would have seen a mane of

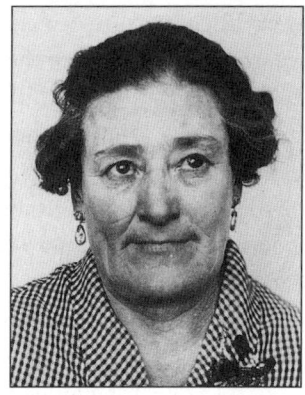

Mug shots of Eva Dugan, circa late 1920s.

flaming red hair with a slash of steel gray at the part line. She often wore a bun at the back with a tortoise comb and was usually seen in shell-rimmed spectacles.

Tried, convicted and sentenced, Eva was sent off to Florence to do a three- to six-year term for auto theft, all the while proclaiming her innocence and insisting the elusive Jack had stolen the car. The Mathis disappearance nagged at authorities, and the investigation continued at full steam. Finally, the big break came.

On December 23, 1927, a traveling Californian named J. F. Nash selected a secluded spot on the Mathis ranch as a suitable place to camp. Efforts to drive a tent post into the ground were stymied by a hard object. Assuming it was a rock, Nash dug around it. What the digging revealed was not a rock but the yellowed skull of a human being. Police were summoned, and the skeletal remains of Andrew J. Mathis were removed from the shallow grave where they had rested nearly a year. Identification was made by papers in the clothing and a set of dentures. At last, murder charges could be brought against Eva.

The Mathis killing was one of the most talked-about murder cases in years. The public clamored for each tidbit of rumor, gossip, and innuendo and read every word printed about the accused woman. Court convened February 21, 1928, and, for so spectacular a case, was of remarkably short duration—just five days. During three of those days, the victim's skull was on display in the courtroom. Among those asked to identify it was a former neighbor, a woman who testified the skull bore a "close resemblance" to the head of Mathis, and the dead man's barber, who testified he had taken "particular notice" of the shape of the skull. It was hardly the testimony of expert witnesses.

No one had witnessed the crime; the murder weapon had not been found; fingerprints were not available. Virtually all of the evidence used against her was circumstantial, but Eva would prove to be her own worst enemy. Her testimony was disjointed, rambling, contradictory, and nonsensical. She even went so far as to produce a postcard "signed" by Jack absolving her of any wrongdoing. Incapable of telling the same story the same way twice, Eva's credibility suffered irretrievable damage.

At 9:40 P.M., February 25, 1928, after deliberating less than three hours, the jury found Eva guilty of murder in the first degree. The verdict specified the death penalty. This was thought to be the first time in Arizona it had been meted out on circumstantial evidence. The convicted murderess, pale and shaky, leaned forward in her chair but made no outcry, no comment. Her stolid demeanor would become the stuff of legends.

Eva was returned to the prison at Florence, but this time she was incarcerated on death row. In that atmosphere of gloom and uncertainty, she would spend the better part of two years while her lawyers and a handful of supporters worked behind the scenes to effectuate a commutation of her sentence to life in prison. During that time, she would become a favorite of the press, who would suggest she was witty, warm, gracious, and without self-pity.

But no one could help Eva—not her lawyers, not her supporters, not the press, not even Governor John C. Phillips. On February 15, 1930, six days before her scheduled execution, all hope of a commutation was abandoned. "My hands are tied," Phillips told the Associated Press. "The law does not empower me to grant a reprieve or commutation.... [A] sanity hearing is the condemned woman's only hope."

In a last-ditch effort, Mrs. Allie Dickerman and Mrs. John H. Durham, both well-connected Tucsonans, made a public appeal for funds to support a sanity hearing. The next day, it was announced that they had raised sixty-four dollars. But funds were not all that was necessary. Pinal County attorney Ernest W. McFarland (later, majority leader of the U. S. Senate, governor of Arizona, and Arizona Supreme Court justice) would have to be convinced that the enterprise had merit.

The next day, Dr. Charles W. Brown, former prison physician, signed an affidavit attesting that Eva was, indeed, insane. In quick order, prison warden Lorenzo Wright, former warden Scott White, prison physician Dr. L. A. Love, and Phoenix psychiatrist Dr. Win Wylie all signed affidavits attesting to insanity. A Florence physician, Dr. George Huffman, added his opinion that Eva's health was so precarious she would die within a couple of years at best. He said she had suffered from a "social" disease—then a polite term for syphilis—for thirty years or more and was a very sick woman. McFarland was persuaded, and a sanity hearing was scheduled.

"As an eleventh-hour means of snatching the fifty-two-year-old woman from the grim and inexorable grip of the noose," wrote Gilbert Cosulich in the February 16, 1930, issue of the *Tucson Daily Citizen*, "her two young attorneys have secured an insanity trial for her." The hearing was scheduled for February 18, three days before Eva's scheduled execution.

Ruth Hale, vice president of the American League to Abolish Capital Punishment and wife of distinguished *New York Evening Telegram* critic Heywood Broun, was in Tucson to visit her son, Heywood Hale, a student at the Arizona Desert School. Soon she was in the act, telling reporters, "It is a horrible thing to take a human being and, with measured step, lead him or her to the shambles as one might do an ox or a lamb." That said, she whisked her son off on a vacation in California.

Mrs. Leroy Miller, another Tucsonan, jumped into the fray but in the opposite camp. She told the press she would devote all of her time and strength to circulating a petition to counteract the activities of the Anti-Capital Punishment League, contending that the "sentimental" appeal on behalf of the murderess was a "disgrace."

Dickerman and Durham countered. "Due to the fact that there was not an eye witness to the crime and that ... Eva Dugan has consistently maintained her innocence to the last," they told a gathering of reporters, hoping their words would reach the authorities, "we feel the facts and evidence rendered in the case are not sufficient to warrant the supreme penalty or sacrifice, therefore we pray that you will grant clemency in the case."

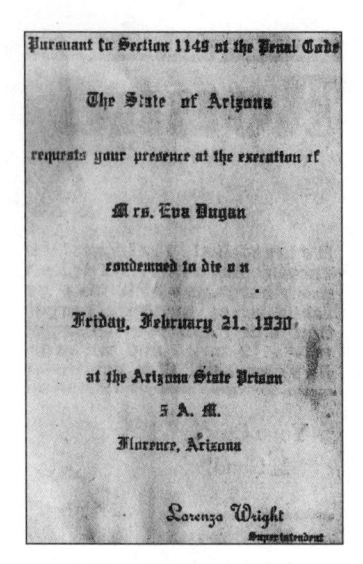

Invitation to Eva Dugan's hanging, Friday, February 21, 1930.

The sanity hearing got under way as scheduled, and, according to the *Arizona Daily Star*, McFarland conducted "a withering cross-examination of witnesses called by the Dugan counsel and entered upon the taking of testimony for the state with only one sworn witness, a prison guard in charge of the condemned woman, who was not called to the stand."

It was all for naught. A jury of twelve men judged Eva sane. With three days left to live, she was little more than a walking corpse. The public continued to agitate on both sides of the issue, those loudest in favor of sparing Eva's life. "I say keep her away from society, but don't hang her on circumstantial evidence," wrote Mrs. J. J. Butterfield of Coolidge, Arizona, to the *Star* the day after the sanity hearing. "Why, the poor, half-witted wretch, she is to be pitied, for she surely is demented."

As the controversy raged, Eva—very much in command of her ego—removed her shell-rimmed spectacles, clasped her hands behind her back, poked out her chin, and grinned (or smirked?) at newspaper photographers. The photo is that of an obese, middle-aged woman not without vanity. Her flaming red hair is neatly coifed. Covering her bulk is a paisley dress, sleeveless and stylishly cut in the day's fashion. Her neck is accented by a bauble dangling to her midsection. Ribbons adorn her shoes. Her appearance is in stark contrast to the bars looming in windows behind her. It would be Eva's last formal portrait.

The day of reckoning arrived, and Gilbert Cosulich, writing for the February 21, 1930, issue of the *Tucson Daily Citizen*, said, "Jauntly swinging her guard's hand as does a maid who goes a-Maying with her swain, Eva Dugan this morning approached her rendezvous with death with a light step and a lighter laugh."

Writing for the same paper, Harold G. Wilson was only slightly less romantic. "She walked to her doom with the courage and wanton abandon which marked her activities during the night, when she smoked cigarettes, played cards, chatted freely with visitors and mildly and nonchalantly affirmed her innocence."

Whether "jauntly swinging" or expressing "wanton abandon," Eva may well have wanted to cheat the gallows by taking her own life. Two women prisoners who refused to reveal their names told an unknown reporter for the Miami, Arizona, *Silver Belt* that Eva admitted having in her possession a razor and a bottle of poison. "Would you want a rope, or would you do something else?" she is reputed to have asked the women. According to the story, the women encouraged her to face her execution bravely.

Acting on a tip, probably from one or both of the women, Warden Lorenzo Wright transferred Eva to the condemned cell at about one o'clock in the morning. The razor was not reported found, but a search of the cell turned up a two-ounce bottle of "deadly poison" bearing the label of a Florence drugstore. The gallows would not be cheated. Eva would remain alive another four hours until the hangman's noose was tightened.

Sometime during the night, a telegram arrived from South Bend, Indiana. It read:

> My dear mother:
> Be brave.... God is with you. All my love. I will pray for you always.

Sent by the condemned woman's daughter, it was the first communication Eva had had from her offspring since her troubles began. It brought her as close to the breaking point as anything would. Still, the woman put forth a stolid demeanor.

The small, drab room on the second floor would be used on the morning of February 21, 1930.

The room had been built to accommodate a scaffold, the condemned criminal, those people necessary to the execution, and twenty-five spectators. But things were different that morning. One newspaper account suggests sixty-five spectators gathered in the room. Another puts the count at seventy-five. Yet another insists eighty people packed themselves into a room designed to hold less than a third that number. Whichever count is accurate, it is certain that the onlookers—whose intentions were many and varied—would not only satisfy a morbid curiosity but would carry away memories they would take to the grave.

According to the United Press (UP), Eva donned a "silken shroud" she had sewn in her prison cell. Accompanied by a guard, she climbed thirteen steps from her cell to the death chamber. Then, with a guard on each side of her, she stepped the few feet to the scaffold. Her shell-rimmed spectacles were removed and a black hood placed over her head. Warden Wright, according to the Associated Press, clasped her hand and said, "God bless you, Eva."

A few seconds later, a steel trap was sprung, and everything—everything went wrong. Eva's body plummeted to the floor below. Eva's head did not. In a split second, it had detached from the torso and then was flung to the floor. It rolled across the room, splattering blood on the feet of horrified spectators. One report says four women fainted. Everyone there was shocked and stunned.

At this writing, Eva Dugan is the only woman to have been executed in Arizona. She was the first woman executed west of the Mississippi River and the twenty-third woman executed in the United States.

June 12, 1930, under the headline "Undesirable Publicity," the *Arizona Daily Star* lamented a new song titled "The Hanging of Eva Dugan" as unfavorable to the good name of Arizona. "According to *Variety*, the leading theatrical journal," said the article, "this lyric lament has attained remarkable sales."

Tenacious even in death, Eva would not go away quietly.

Chapter 3

The Notorious Mail Bandit

MORE THAN 250 INMATES of the McNeil Island Federal Penitentiary stood about in the prison yard on a day early in September 1921, watching a baseball game. All at once, three team members bolted from the field and dashed to the high chain-link fence surrounding the compound. Edward Impyn, serving a life sentence, was shot dead in his tracks. Another lifer, Lawardus Bogart, was wounded as he approached the fence and was taken into custody. The most nimble-footed of the three, Roy P. Gardner, serving a fifty-year sentence for two mail robberies, took a bullet in the leg but nonetheless scaled the fence and vanished into the island's heavily wooded interior.

Located in Puget Sound, not far from Tacoma, Washington, McNeil was a small island just twelve miles square with a civilian population of some seven hundred. The mainland was more than a mile distant across rough waters, and authorities reasoned that without assistance of confederates, there was little chance of Gardner's escaping the island.

An immediate search was taken up. McNeil's residents were warned to be on the lookout for the disappearance of edibles, and every boat on the island was checked. All were accounted for, which added substance to the theory that Gardner was still on the island. Lawmen predicted his capture was just hours away.

They were mistaken.

The thirty-seven-year-old escapee had been out for two days when his wife, Dolly, thirteen years his junior and a department store clerk living in Napa, California, was interviewed by the Associated Press. "He is a daredevil swimmer," she declared. "I have seen him swim far out into the sea...and return in three-quarters of a hour not a bit tired and full of pep."

Dolly also told the reporter she believed "he escaped this time just to show the officers he could do it. He may even wait a while and return to the prison and say, 'Here I am, warden.'"

Dolly was both right and wrong. Gardner, who had escaped confinement twice before, would not return voluntarily to the penitentiary. But, contrary to his trackers' belief, he had reached the mainland by swimming the choppy swells of Puget Sound.

During the early evening of November 15, 1921, seventy-one days after Gardner's daring escape, a masked gunman jumped aboard the mail car on train number 170 of the Atchison, Topeka and Santa Fe Railway as it was about to depart the Santa Fe depot in Phoenix on its run to Los Angeles.

On an adjacent track was a Southern Pacific train, its mail car guarded by two U. S. Marines. Earlier, Herman Inderlied, since 1910 a mail clerk for the Atchison, Topeka and Santa Fe, was asked by the postmaster if he wanted a marine guard. "No," he replied, "I'll be my own marine."

His words were prophetic.

Inderlied followed his routine of taking the mail to the train by truck, then loading it into the car. That task completed, he removed his gun and tossed it onto a table, locked the car's door, and changed his clothes. Then he walked to the mailbox at the corner of the station platform and returned with a handful of letters. When he reentered the car, the masked gunman stepped out of the shadows and told him to put up his hands. Inderlied refused, whereupon the man forced him at gunpoint to the rear of the car and ordered him to lie on his belly.

The mail clerk complied with the assailant's command, but he had not the slightest intention of letting a robbery occur. At his first opportunity, he seized the gunman's wrist and threw him off balance. At the same time, he grabbed the man's hair and forced him to the floor—all the while calling out for help.

The men wrestled, and Inderlied—who was six feet, two inches tall and tipped the scale at 215 pounds—managed to subdue his attacker and take possession of the gun. He then sat atop the intruder until Phoenix policeman Nick Papo and Santa Fe Special Agent Lewis J. Swarnes came to his assistance and took the bandit into custody. Just then a whistle blew, the brakeman hollered all aboard, and there was the familiar sound of loosening brakes.

As though nothing out of the ordinary had occurred, Inderlied turned his attention away from the would-be robber and went about his duties in the mail car. In another moment, he was on his way to Los Angeles.

As the captive was taken away, he turned to the slowly moving mail car and shouted, "You've caught me all right, and I guess you know that means a five-thousand-dollar reward. And I guess you know you sure earned it tonight."

It was odd for a failed holdup man to compliment his captor.

Then the bandit was whisked away to the Phoenix police station, where he was photographed, fingerprinted, and locked in a cell. He gave his name as R. P. Nelson and claimed to be from Chicago. Law-enforcement authorities were skeptical.

The next day, fingerprints and a wanted poster revealed that R. P. Nelson was in fact Roy P. Gardner, a fugitive from justice eagerly sought by federal authorities.

The prisoner was quickly arraigned in U. S. District Court, and bond was set at a whopping $100,000. When asked the customary question regarding his ability to furnish such a sum, the prisoner smiled and said, "I think I can make it."

Lawmen thought little about it at the time, but Gardner had established a pattern. His smile would be perpetual, his bluster frequent. Raising a $100,000 bond fell into the latter category, and he was locked away again.

Following the arraignment, The *Arizona Republican* (now the *Republic*) reported that "any opportunity to try [Gardner] in Phoenix ... was wiped away ... when Thomas A. Flynn, United States district attorney here, and Joseph P. Dillon, United States marshal, were ordered to send Gardner to the federal penitentiary at Leavenworth, Kansas, where he will again begin to serve the fifty-year sentence which is hanging over him because of two former mail robberies.

"Word of the identification of the prisoner had been scattered throughout the city, and perhaps the largest crowd that ever attended a preliminary hearing here was on hand to look at the well-known prisoner."

Then, in prose more suited to covering stars of the silver screen, the newspaper noted that "Gardner was dressed in a blue suit with a khaki colored woolen shirt. His 196 pounds of bone and muscle were apparent in his broad shoulders and fine physical condition; and his face ruddy and healthy in appearance, wore a genial smile during the entire proceedings."

Gardner's geniality and smiling demeanor played well in the press. Hundreds of sentences would be written about his good humor, and the public would cling to every word.

Words that authorities wanted to hear were forthcoming when the uninhibited prisoner told of his escape from the penitentiary at McNeil Island.

After his dash to freedom, the escapee had hidden for three days under his guards' noses in the prison barn. There he lived on milk from a nearby herd of dairy cows. When he grew weary of that routine, Gardner ventured into the woods, where he spent two days. At last, the bullet wound in his leg healed sufficiently, and he slipped into the waters of Puget Sound and swam to the mainland.

He wandered down the coast to Raymond, Washington, where he stole an automobile and drove to Portland, Oregon. From there, he made many stops along the coast until he reached Napa, California, where he visited his wife and four-year-old daughter. He told Dolly he would flee into Mexico, where he would be free of the United States.

But it was not to be. He went to Mexicali but found it not to his liking. Soon he was back in the states, traveling to Phoenix via Yuma and Maricopa—then a major terminus on the railroad.

Interviewed again by an AP reporter, Dolly said, "I don't know whether to be glad or sorry, or what to think. It was so horrible, just when I thought he was safe. I will rearrange my plans to be near him, wherever that may be."

Meantime, the western superintendent of railway mail service announced that Inderlied would indeed receive the reward of five thousand dollars offered for the capture of anyone who attempted to rob the mails and, perhaps, also a two-thousand-dollar reward offered for the capture of Gardner—no trifling sum for a mail clerk acting as his own marine.

"For several hours yesterday the county jail and the sheriff's office became the center of attraction in Phoenix," reported the *Republican*. "Both men and women crowded about the building and the corridors of the sheriff's office in an effort to catch a glimpse of the famous bandit."

The same day, a reporter noted that Gardner, "sitting on the edge of the table in his cell ... swung his foot back and forth and laughed out from behind the bars. In the dim light he looked like a moving picture artist playing the part of a much wronged hero, and playing it well. His hair was brushed back at just the right angle from his well formed forehead and his eyes glinted with just the right amount of pathos at the proper moment. He also has the moving picture trick of running his fingers through his thick locks and making them ripple and curl."

Gushing with descriptiveness, the writer continued, "There are crinkles of laughter around his eyes and his large, humorous mouth is forever stretching into a laugh as he talks, for care sits very lightly on Roy Gardner's shoulders."

"Well, Roy," inquired the sheriff after Gardner was turned over to his care, "do you intend to try to escape from this jail?"

"Certainly, I do," answered the prisoner. "Wouldn't you, if you had seventy-five years staring you in the face?"

"We shoot to kill here," the sheriff told him.

"That's all in the game," came Gardner's glib reply.

The next day, November 18, a new twist developed when the AP reported that "police and post office inspectors today announced that they had secured evidence implicating Roy Gardner ... in the mail robbery at Maricopa, Arizona, November 3."

The *Republican* took up the story: "Two mail robberies, in all probability, will be checked up against Roy Gardner, spectacular mail bandit, whose escapes from police authorities have made his name a household word throughout the United States. ... Positive proof that Gardner robbed ... [a] mail car at Maricopa on November 3 of ... [several] pouches of registered mail has been uncovered by post office authorities."

While the mail heist at Maricopa would figure prominently in Gardner's story, nothing more was heard about the second robbery mentioned in the *Republican* article.

On the heels of that announcement came a report that orders had been received by U. S. District Attorney Flynn from the attorney general's office to prosecute Gardner in Phoenix for his attempt to rob the Santa Fe mail car.

"The change of attitude, according to Attorney Flynn, was taken because of the desire of the government that Herman F. Inderlied, the railway mail clerk who captured Gardner, should receive the reward of five thousand dollars offered by the post office department."

Apparently, had Gardner been sent directly to Leavenworth without having been tried in Arizona, a glitch in the law would have denied Inderlied the reward money.

The *Republican* noted that Gardner had dined at the American Kitchen cafe with Marshal Dillon, who, he said, was an "admirable" host. "The general public," said Gardner, "is made up of funny people. When the diners ... became aware of the fact that I was in there, they became all eyes. I could feel them looking at me and when I would look up, suddenly they would try their best not to appear to be looking."

Then, in a statement quite out of character, Gardner added, "I really think ... that the American people show too much sympathy for the man in jail for the good of the country."

It was a remarkable statement from the lips of a man who coveted public attention.

Soon it was learned that behind the capricious side of Gardner's personality rested a mind with intriguing bends. "Is Roy Gardner a religious fanatic, is he insane or is he merely the daredevil bandit who rather glories in being the best known criminal in the United States?" the *Republican* asked its readers. "He gives evidence of being any and all of these characters, say the federal and county officials and the scores of persons who ... have been permitted to interview him in his cell....

"The theory that he is a religious fanatic who is 'controlled by those who have gone ahead' is being advanced by the many who are firm in the conviction that the man ... is guided by the influence of the departed."

Gardner told authorities that his mother was a "materializing spiritualist," and admitted that, just prior to her death, she had been pronounced insane.

It then was revealed that "Dr. Thomas R. Haines of New York, who is conducting a mental hygiene survey of Arizona, [will] visit [Gardner] in his cell."

When Dolly arrived in Phoenix on November 20, the *Republican* turned to its thesaurus in search of flattering words. "Mrs. Gardner is an unusually attractive and pretty blonde," wrote the newspaper. "Her features are regular and her complexion is of the real peaches-and-cream type. Her twenty-four years—five of which have been spent as the wife of Roy Gardner—rest easily on her, and she seems even younger than she is. Dressed smartly but unobtrusively, she presented a trim picture...."

"Marshal Dillon admitted...that when she stood before his desk...he had to think twice before he had erased from his mind his preconceived idea of what Gardner's wife should look like."

After a lengthy visit with her husband, Dolly was accosted by reporters. "Roy was always good to me," she told them, "and I was happy with him. I did not know when I married him that he had already served a prison sentence, but I do not think that this would have made any difference. I knew only that he was restless, and I hoped that after a while he would settle down...."

"Roy is not bad at heart, and he is not lazy," she declared, adding that she could not condone his crimes but did not think the bandit was "exactly normal mentally." She said the first mail robbery occurred when he was "broke," and subsequent offenses had been the result of a "need for food."

"We never quarreled," she added. "He never has given me a cross word. He always got up with a smile and he went to bed with a smile. He was simply crazy about little Jean, our daughter.

"I suppose if he hadn't been so good to me I wouldn't be sticking with him now. Still, I know he'd stick to me if I were in trouble, and it's up to me to do the same...[for] him."

The press now had two people to fawn over, and every move made by Dolly was covered in breathless detail.

Wrote the *Republican*, "From the time when she entered the city...she had won the esteem and respect of all with whom she has come in contact. Pretty and attractive in dress and manner; unassuming and without any appearance of pose; soft of voice and prepossessing in her attitude to those who she met during the day, she proved that she is just what she looks to be—a home-loving little woman who is doing everything in her power for a husband who, despite his failings, has retained her affection through every vicissitude."

While much ado was being made in the press about Gardner and his wife, U. S. district attorney Flynn was hard at work building a case in the Maricopa train robbery.

On November 3, the mail car of train number 203 of the Arizona Eastern Railway had been robbed of several pouches of registered mail. Within a few hours, the greater part of the loot had been found—most of which consisted of insurance papers and other matter of little use to anyone except the sender and the receiver. The single item of real value was a lady's wristwatch belonging to a Hayden, Arizona, woman.

With investigators using the watch as a basis, evidence slowly unfolded. Gardner stated upon his arrest that he had been in Phoenix twenty-four days. Backtracking to October 22, officers learned that he had registered that day at the Bachelors Inn. His movements then were traced to Casa Grande and back to Phoenix.

Before the case went to trial, Flynn offered a chronological outline of the evidence he would present:

October 22. Gardner registered at the Bachelors Inn, 144 East Adams Street, and was given room nine. He remained at the inn that night only.

October 28. Gardner was on the east-bound Southern Pacific train to Casa Grande.

October 31. Gardner went to the shop of Letis R. Templin, a locksmith, and ordered a key made for a Pullman lock. Templin told him that he could not make a key without the lock. Gardner left and returned in half an hour with the lock, whereupon Templin made the key, charging Gardner one dollar. Gardner left with both lock and key.

November 1. Gardner reregistered at the Bachelors Inn. He was given room eleven and remained only one night.

November 3. The Arizona Eastern Railway mail car was robbed at Maricopa.

November 4. Gardner reregistered at the Bachelors Inn. He was given room nine, and paid $2.50 in advance. He lodged at the inn until the botched Santa Fe robbery November 15.

November 10. Gardner exhibited to Mrs. Gillespie, housekeeper at the Bachelors Inn, a lady's wristwatch and expressed a desire to obtain a ten-dollar loan on it.

November 11. Gardner gave the same watch to Mrs. Collins, proprietor of the Bachelors Inn and Kelly's Waffle Kitchen, as security for meals and lodging.

November 15. Gardner was apprehended while trying to rob the Santa Fe mail car.

November 17. The watch was recovered by officers from Mrs. Collins.

November 18. The lock on the Arizona Eastern mail car was identified by locksmith Templin as the same lock Gardner had brought to him on October 31.

November 19. A key was found on the top of a joist in room nine of the Bachelors Inn. It was identified by Templin as the key he had made for Gardner on October 31. Gardner apparently had cut the lock on the Eastern Arizona mail car, replaced it with his own, then waited until a propitious time to commit the robbery.

On November 23 Gardner was indicted on two charges of mail robbery and bound over for trial on December 5. To no one's surprise, he entered a plea of not guilty. Quite surprising, however, was a written plea entered by his attorney, Carl A. Davis, stating that Gardner's defense would be based upon allegations of insanity. "Said defendant is not guilty of the offense charged against him," wrote Davis, "for reasons that at the time referred to in the indictment he was mentally unsound and did not have criminal intent."

Three days later, Gardner was taken to a laboratory, where x-ray photographs were made of his head "with particular reference to an injury sustained by the prisoner about twelve years ago in Bisbee when he was struck on the head during a strike in the mining camp," wrote the *Republican.* "His injury . . . had resulted in a depression upon the brain which for several years subjected Gardner to epileptic attacks."

Hospital records at Bisbee showed that a man named Gardner had indeed sustained a fractured skull on March 26, 1908, and was admitted to the Copper Queen Mining Company hospital, where he remained until April 6.

Gardner's insanity plea did nothing to temper the *Republican's* rhapsodic prose. "He appears to be the most jovial prisoner in jail and is always ready to talk to anyone willing to talk to him." The newspaper noted that each day women, wishing to glimpse the prisoner, were turned away.

On November 30 Mauk's Columbia Theatre announced that in addition to its regular fare of silent movies, "original views of Roy Gardner" would grace its screen. "Included in these views are pictures of Gardner on his way to the federal court room . . . Gardner talking to his wife, playing cards with cell mates, and conversing with his attorney." The announcement noted that Gardner "is . . . [a] most picturesque bandit."

Gardner's trial opened December 5 in U. S. District Court, Judge William H. Swatelle presiding. U. S. district attorney Flynn announced that the Maricopa mail robbery would be tried first, and jury selection began. Twenty-nine prospective jurors were questioned, and from that number, twelve men were selected—women were not then allowed to sit on Arizona juries.

After pleas were read, Flynn presented testimony concerning the lady's wristwatch stolen from the mail at Maricopa and given to the proprietor of the Bachelors Inn as security. He presented a sworn statement from Mrs. E. P. Janney to the effect that she had sent the watch via registered mail from Salt Lake City on October 31 to Mrs. B. E. Phillips, her sister-in-law and a resident of Hayden. Phillips then testified that she had lent the watch to Janney when the latter had visited Arizona. When shown the watch, she made a positive identification.

It was damning testimony, and the next afternoon the government rested its case.

It then was Carl Davis' turn to present a defense he hoped would convince the jury of his client's alleged insanity. The first witness called to the stand was L. R. Barrow, postmaster at San Diego when Gardner committed his first mail robbery on April 28, 1920.

The *Republican* took up the story: "A post office inspector, the witness said, showed Mrs. Gardner in her husband's presence a circular from San Quentin penitentiary describing Gardner, who had served two years of a five years sentence there after having been convicted of the robbery of a jewelry store in San Francisco. Gardner was pardoned after having quelled a revolt among the prisoners on Christmas Eve of 1912.

"When the circular was shown to Mrs. Gardner she swooned, the witness said, while Gardner rolled his eyes, appeared very excited and then gave the appearance of not being interested at all in the incident or his wife."

Dolly was the next witness to testify. After a lengthy recital in which she detailed the years of their marriage, she told of Gardner's belief in spirits, his fear of the dark, his superstitions, and his desire for publicity and notoriety. She said he had tried to develop his "mediumship," which, he believed, he possessed to an "uncommon degree" and like his mother was a firm believer in "spiritual guides." Dolly concluded her testimony by declaring that she had known since she married the accused that Gardner was mentally unsound at times and that he had become gradually worse over the years.

A man who had worked with Gardner at the mines in Mammoth related several instances of his "abnormality," and an ex-convict from San Quentin testified that Gardner had "twice fallen into fits."

The following day, Gardner took the stand in his own defense. He told the court that he considered nothing but murder a crime—that he was not amenable to man-made laws, "which have no place in the spiritual plane."

Gardner told of his birth in Missouri, of a move to Colorado at age eleven, of finishing high school, and of working the mines in Colorado, New Mexico, Arizona, and old Mexico—also of the head injury sustained in Bisbee, which had resulted in surgery.

In his youth, he had attended the Methodist Church, but his mother's "mediumship" compelled him to study the principals of spiritualism with her. Together, they held séances and attended spiritualist conventions. He said he could see and hear spirits and since childhood had had two "controls"—Wareeka and White Feather.

In cross-examination, Flynn asked him if the mail robberies had been committed after consulting with the spirits.

"Whatever I've done has been done by my physical body," replied Gardner.

"Have you a mind?"

"Certainly."

"What spirit did you consult?"

"Wareeka always advised against it."

"Did you consult your controls . . . [before the escape from] McNeil Island?"

"White Feather."

"Is White Feather a good control?"

"Good and bad. He said that I would not be injured, nor would I 'pass on.' Either he was under another control or he gave me a bum steer, for I was wounded."

Reiterating that he did not believe in man-made laws, Gardner was interrupted by Judge Swatelle, who asked him, "Do I understand that if you were acquitted of all the charges against you, you would consider yourself at liberty to go out and rob right and left?"

"Judge Swatelle," replied Gardner, "I am not amenable to your law, and I am not going to be on this plane very long anyhow. I have no respect for the law."

And that concluded Gardner's testimony.

The next witness, a physician, testified regarding the x-ray photographs taken the previous week of Gardner's head. The photos, he said, revealed an unusually thick skull, which seemed to have thickened even more at the point where the accused had been struck in Bisbee.

Virtually all testimony the following day centered on an examination of Gardner's sanity by experts called by the defense. They agreed unanimously that the defendant was unbalanced.

It was then that Judge Swatelle made the most important ruling of the day—one that would influence the course of the entire proceeding. "You must not connect Gardner's belief in spiritualism," he told the jury, "with the particular act charged in the indictment. Men of the highest intellectual development . . . [such] as Sir Oliver Lodge and Sir Arthur Conan Doyle, leaders in the fields of science and letters, believe in spiritualism, and to call these men insane would be absurd."

Swatelle instructed the sanity experts to "eliminate from your answers . . . any reference to spiritualism which is either for or against the defendant."

It was a crippling blow to Gardner's insanity plea.

It then was revealed to the court that after his escape from McNeil Island, Gardner had written a letter to President Warren G. Harding begging for a pardon "to prove to the world that a criminal can reform and be an asset to society and a good husband and father."

The letter had been turned over to the postmaster general, then to the attorney general. While Gardner awaited a reply, the postmaster general told the press there would be no compromise with mail bandits. Soon after the statement was made, the defendant was back in the business of mail robbery.

On December 11 the defense rested its case and placed Gardner's fate in the hands of the jury. Eighteen hours later, the foreman reported that they were hopelessly deadlocked. Swatelle dismissed them, after which Flynn announced that Gardner would be brought to trial again—the very next morning.

The *Republican* editorialized that "we do not think that one who followed the testimony closely could have believed that the defendant was insane, that is, much more insane than the rest of us."

The public was stunned when, on the following day, Gardner appeared before Judge Swatelle and pleaded guilty to the charges of assaulting Herman Inderlied and attempting to rob the Santa Fe mail car. In the blink of an eye, Swatelle sentenced him to serve twenty-five years in the federal penitentiary at Leavenworth, a penalty that was not discretionary on the part of the judge but was fixed by federal law for assault with a deadly weapon upon a mail clerk.

In addition to the most recent sentence, Gardner already faced seventy-five years behind bars. But Swatelle, bending ever so slightly, told the prisoner that he need not serve the entire sentence. "If you change your mental attitude concerning the laws of this country," he said, "and you gain different ideas of the rights of others, especially with regard to property, I feel confident that you will have the chance someday to be a good citizen, both for your own sake and for the sake of your wife, who has stood by you in this case, thus demonstrating her love and loyalty to you."

Flynn then moved that the charge against Gardner of having robbed the Arizona Eastern Railway mail car at Maricopa be dismissed. This was done.

Before he was taken back to the county jail, Gardner promised Marshal

Dillon that he would make no attempt to escape or to make trouble of any kind before reaching Leavenworth, and he gave post office inspectors a diagram showing where he had concealed three registered-mail pouches in the desert near Maricopa.

On December 13, in the custody of Dillon and three other officers, the man the press called the "notorious mail bandit" was on a train bound for Kansas. The historical record does not indicate whether, because of Gardner's presence on the train, special guards were placed aboard the mail car. But one can speculate.

Chapter 4

Bad Days on the Kaibab

IT WAS A MORNING in 1930 when Buck Lowrey, owner of the trading post at Marble Canyon on the northwestern lip of the vast Navajo Indian Reservation, spotted two young boys walking toward his modest cafe and filling station—not a common sight at such a remote outpost. Engaging the youths in conversation, he learned they were brothers, Carl and Albert White, twelve and fourteen years of age respectively. After a bit of coaxing, the lads admitted they had run away from the family farm in Provo, Utah, a straight-laced Mormon community some fifty miles south of the more cosmopolitan capital at Salt Lake City. Himself a father, Buck was concerned, and sensing their immediate need, he treated the brothers to a free meal, all the while gently nudging them to agree to return home. At last, the boys acknowledged their folly. Buck found a sympathetic tourist, who drove them to the sheriff's office at Flagstaff, where transportation to Utah was arranged.

Satisfied he had acted in the youngsters' best interests, Buck went about his work and put the incident out of his mind. But half a decade later, his memory would be stirred in dramatic fashion.

The White brothers, now aged seventeen and nineteen, chose the summer of 1935 to abandon the farm again. This time their modus operandi was more sophisticated. They did not put out their thumbs but stole an automobile—not just any automobile but a brand-new Dodge sedan from a Provo dealership.

An odyssey unfolded that would take them through Wyoming, Montana, Wyoming again, Colorado, and New Mexico. Driving on pilfered Wyoming license plates, they met travel expenses by robbing out-of-the-way post offices. Somewhere between Gallup, New Mexico, and Holbrook,

Arizona, they picked up a hitchhiker named Carl Cox, a young man from Indiana possessed of an amoral nature compatible with their own. The trio then drove the stolen vehicle through Arizona with the notion of returning to central Utah.

At Cedar Ridge, a tiny blip on the map north of the Navajo trading post at Cameron, they stopped long enough to terrorize two women tourists and steal $150 in traveler's checks.

Late that evening, their automobile crossed the Colorado River over Navajo Bridge and pulled into the Marble Canyon Trading Post a quarter mile north. The young men knew the traveler's checks would be problematic and wanted to replenish their cash supply. Given its remote location, the trading post looked like an easy target for a holdup.

Buck and his twenty-five-year-old son, David, had turned in for the night, leaving an aged Englishman, William G. Wilson, in charge of the filling station. Wilson, a man of few words who revealed little about himself, had migrated to Marble Canyon from California eighteen months earlier and served the business as a kind of jack-of-all-trades. Buck considered him a devoted employee.

When the delinquents drove up, Wilson was busy with another motorist's auto. Killing time, the young men asked where they could put air in a tire. Wilson indicated a nearby pump. They pulled the car over, got out, and fiddled a moment with its tires, then loitered about drinking soda pop while they waited for the old man to finish up. As soon as the other car

Buck Lowrey's Filling Station; Marble Canyon, circa 1930.

David and father, Buck Lowrey, circa 1935.

drove off, Albert thrust a gun into Wilson's midsection and demanded money. "Put up your hands," he is reported to have said in Hollywood fashion. "It's a holdup."

But the loyal Wilson took umbrage at the notion of relinquishing the night's receipts. Rather than comply, he swung at Albert with a flashlight. It would be a fatal error. The Utah farm boy pulled the revolver's trigger and blew a hole in the Englishman's belly. In terrific pain but resolute in his resistance, the wounded man clutched at his midsection and started for a back room, where a gun was cached. But it was all for naught. "His assailant followed and shot again as Wilson got his hand on the gun," the June 28, 1935, issue of the *Coconino Sun* would report, "but the bullet went wild."

The boys were unnerved. Robbing small-town post offices and female tourists was one thing; putting a bullet into a man's flesh was quite another. "I got the gun by the . . . [barrel]," Wilson later told Coconino County attorney Karl Mangum, "and by the time I got straightened out, the man who shot me ran back to the car, and they all drove away." As the stolen Dodge fled north, the wounded man made his way to the side of the highway and emptied his gun at the disappearing auto.

In moments, Buck and his son were up and about. Gunfire on their property was not something to be taken lightly. Finding Wilson in a critical state, they acted quickly and decisively. They arranged to have him driven to the Indian hospital at Tuba City—an agonizing journey over rutted dirt roads—then piled into their automobile and sped off in the direction of the perpetrators. But they made a costly mistake. Neither man had checked the vehicle's fuel level. Soon they were at the side of the road, out of gas, frustrated, and losing precious time. After a wrenching delay, they flagged down a passing motorist and pressed its driver for fuel, then proceeded some forty miles to Jacob Lake on the Kaibab Plateau.

Recognizing the futility of a delayed pursuit, Buck telephoned sometime deputy sheriff Tom Jensen at Fredonia, the tiny Mormon farming community three miles south of the Utah border. Rousted from sleep, Jensen pulled on his trousers, called in help, and in a short time had thrown up a barricade across U. S. Highway 89.

This happened not a moment too soon. Minutes later, Albert, Carl, and their hitchhiking companion approached the barricade at full throttle. Brakes screeched, a hail of bullets rang out, and the fugitives' brown Dodge made a hasty turnabout and sped off in the direction whence it had come. They had escaped into the black of night.

Reports fail to mention why a chase was not immediately taken up, but it is known that Jensen assembled his men in an effort to reassess their position and sort out the next move. Where was the trio? Logic dictated that the boys would not backtrack on the highway to Marble Canyon. They could abandon the car, tackle the desert by foot, and sneak over the Utah line into Kanab. But that seemed like a remote possibility. The best scenario suggested the culprits would take one of many side roads into the thickset pines of the Kaibab forest in an effort to elude the lawmen.

It occurred to Jensen that the road leading past the obscure hamlet of Ryan was the most likely route and, by happenstance, his twenty-four-year-old son, Herman, lived there. The father awakened his son by telephone and learned that indeed an automobile had whizzed by at high speed about two A.M. Jensen chose to remain at the roadblock just in case the boys returned and dispatched two of his men, J. B. Edwards and J. J. Witt, to Ryan with instructions to pick up Herman and begin searching the forest.

Apparently, the White brothers and their Indiana friend felt secure beneath the high pines of the Kaibab. Sometime during the night, they drove the stolen sedan into a clearing, stopped its engine, and nodded off to sleep. It was not a wise decision. At first light, Edwards, Witt, and Herman spotted the automobile. With weapons at the ready, they awakened the trio and demanded they get out of the car with their hands in the air. Instead, the driver—probably Albert—attempted to start the engine. Another bad decision. The lawmen opened fire, and a bullet shattered Carl White's elbow. Recognizing that their situation was untenable, the youths fled the automobile and disappeared into the forest, the White brothers heading west, Cox east.

Later, Carl White would exclaim, "I thought hell had broke lose when those bullets started crashing into the car." It had.

As the hunt was about to resume, Art Vandevier, sheriff of Coconino County, and his chief deputy, Durwood McKinney, arrived on the scene and assumed command. The deputies were more than happy to relinquish decision-making authority to full-time professionals well schooled in police work.

By this time, the lawbreakers had a good head start, and the lawmen knew that the pursuit would be a long, arduous ordeal. Tracking continued throughout the day and the night and into the next day. Then, about mid-morning, McKinney and Herman drew a bead on the White brothers. Hidden beside a boulder at the bottom of a canyon, the boys were fast asleep. They awakened to find the barrels of two rifles pointed at their chests. Smart enough—or frightened enough—not to offer resistance, Albert and Carl gave up the game. Later that day, Cox was captured at Three Lakes, Arizona, some fifteen miles away. He, too, went along without a struggle.

The trio was locked away in the county jail at Flagstaff, all the while proclaiming their innocence. A fourth member of their party had been responsible for the shooting of Wilson, they insisted, but he had bolted from the car just minutes after they escaped the roadblock at Fredonia. Authorities regarded the story as desperate fiction.

Meantime, Albert's victim was transferred from the Indian hospital at Tuba City to Mercy Hospital in Flagstaff; he identified Albert as his assailant. "That's the baby who shot me," he told officers.

"I never told . . . [Wilson] that he was going to die," Buck related to a *Sun* reporter, "because there were no relatives to notify and I thought it best not to worry him." Ten hours later, with Buck at his bedside, the old man took his last breath.

In quick order, the White brothers and Carl Cox were charged with first-degree murder, burglary at nighttime, and robbery. On July 5 the *Sun* reported that "all three signed confessions discarding the yarn about a fourth man."

In a moment of candor, the White brothers told Buck that they were the same boys he had helped in 1930, the first time they had passed through Marble Canyon. Bitter over the murder of Wilson, Buck said, "That's a hell of a way to repay my kindness."

Albert was not enamored of jail and found the prospect of execution unsettling. By one means or another, he smuggled—or had someone smuggle—a hacksaw into his cell and set about the task of sawing apart the bars. On the morning of July 21, he squeezed through a small opening he had created, pried open a window in the jailhouse corridor, and took his leave.

Hours would pass before guards discovered his absence. He lay low during the day and waited until nightfall before stealing a new Ford V-8 sedan, an automobile with the kind of get-up-and-go Albert liked. He had driven the car just a few miles north of Flagstaff on Highway 89 when it rolled to an inelegant stop—out of gas. Precious hours were lost as Albert scoured the countryside seeking fuel. At last, he was on the road again speeding north.

Sheriff Vandevier was not at all happy about the killer's escape and telephoned his counterparts across the Southwest, informing them that the dangerous youth was at large and ought to be put back in jail before he committed further misdeeds. Vandevier also called Buck at Marble Canyon. It would prove to be the most important call the sheriff made.

Buck, himself a deputy, erected a roadblock across the two-lane highway fronting the trading post and put up a sign demanding that all northbound motorists stop their vehicles.

He heard an intriguing anecdote from a breakfasting tourist. The man had been flagged down just north of Flagstaff by a frantic young man in need of gasoline. The fellow was so desperate he offered the driver his spare tire in exchange. The tourist had declined the offer.

Buck's gut instinct told him Albert was on his way. He and his son snatched up weapons—a .35 Remington automatic rifle for Buck and a six-shooter for David—and, bounding into their automobile, sped south across Navajo Bridge.

Buck's instinct was right on target. Some fourteen miles down the road, "they saw a cloud of dust straight ahead a mile and a half away," wrote the *Sun*. As the automobile came toward them at unbridled speed, Buck slammed on his breaks, got out of the car—rifle in hand—and signaled with waving arms for the fast-moving vehicle to pull over. Albert, behind the wheel of the spirited V-8, was not so inclined. Instead, he put his foot to the floor and aimed the speeding automobile directly at Buck.

Buck leaped into a ditch and fired his weapon at the Ford's windshield. Then David opened fire. According to the *Sun*, "The ... car was hidden in a cloud of dust as it careened first toward one side of the road, then ploughing up the gravel, veered across and off the other side, narrowly missing the end post of a long guard rail and bumping, gradually slowing, over rocks to the bottom of the canyon."

Father and son cautiously approached the automobile and peered inside. Albert, the farm boy from Provo, Utah, lay sprawled across the front seat, three bullet holes gaping from his skull. As Buck would tell a coroner's jury, the young man was "very dead."

Riddled with bullet holes, "the getaway car" said the *Sun*, "was towed with its gruesome burden behind the sheriff's car to Flagstaff." Albert's bloody corpse was roped to the seat.

"I can't understand it," said Albert Henry White, father of the killer, who had come to Flagstaff to claim the boy's body. Described as "well dressed and prosperous looking," he told reporters, "When I saw Albert ... [he said] he was going to go straight and try to find a job."

On September 8, 1935, Carl White and Carl Cox went to court. Found guilty of lesser charges, each was sentenced to not less than ten years and not more than fifteen years in the state penitentiary at Florence.

Buck and his son went about the business of running the Marble Canyon Trading Post, hoping to put the bizarre events of the summer behind them. A grateful coroner's jury wrote, "We wish to commend ... [Buck and David Lowrey] for having performed a real service to Coconino County and the state at large."

Chapter 5

Pia and the Peace Officers

CLOUDS OF WAR HUNG HEAVY over the Pacific. Wherever Tucsonans gathered, they discussed and debated the inevitable–participation of the United States as an armed combatant. Isolationists wanted nothing to do with the fighting. Realists knew it was just a matter of time.

In October 1940, fourteen months prior to the bloody attack on Pearl Harbor, more than sixteen million young American men had registered for the draft. Patriotic fever ran high, but here and there holdouts resisted conscription. Among them were a handful of Papago (Tohono O'odham) insulated from world events by their isolation from mainstream society.

Living in the tiny village of Stoa Pitk, located at a remote spot west of Tucson on the vast Papago reservation, these men were led by a venerable old man named Pia Machita–"Man Without a Grindstone." He ruled his village with absolute authority and wanted nothing to do with the white man's notion of civilization. Described by a contemporary reporter as a man of "striking physique," he brandished a cane he claimed had once been owned by Father Eusebio Francisco Kino himself. Refusing to acknowledge the authority of the U. S. government, Pia insisted he and his followers were citizens of Mexico and not subject to what he considered the harassment of health inspectors, census takers, and other bureaucrats who roamed the reservation. "This is my land," he said. "These are my people. White man leave me alone, I leave white man alone."

But the white man had no intention of leaving Pia, his land, or his people alone. Even though illiteracy would prohibit the Papagos from being called up for military service, government officials were adamant that Pia's young men register for the draft. Equally adamant, the old man refused.

A mild hysteria ran through Tucson's extremist element, fueled by the notion that Japan might invade the United States through Mexico and that the Papago would become its allies. However flimsy the reasoning, this fanciful scenario convinced authorities that Pia and his uncooperative braves presented a threat. He and his ragtag band would have to be arrested for draft evasion.

Following a rutted dirt trail across the dusty reservation, U. S. marshal Henry W. Smith arrived at Stoa Pitk about two in the morning with canisters of tear gas. Rousting Pia from sleep, the marshal slapped handcuffs on his wrists and was ready to transport his prisoner to Tucson. But it was not a proposition that sat well with the old man's followers. The Papagos routed the invaders and set their leader free. Smith and his men returned to the city bruised and embarrassed—and without the Papago chief.

Not one to be humiliated by an "illiterate," Smith filed charges. Eight days later, officers stormed the village again, only to return home in frustration. Stoa Pitk was deserted.

It was Deputy Sheriff Ben McKinney who conjured up the most bizarre plan. From the army at Fort Huachuca, he requested a plane, gas bombs, machine guns, and hand grenades. Mercifully, the army exercised prudent judgment, and the request was denied. Nevertheless, another raid was staged. And again the village was deserted.

Six months would pass before the successful invasion of the tiny Native American village. McKinney led the assault, commanding his ground troops from the cockpit of a borrowed airplane. At last, the elusive group of Papagos was arrested and taken into custody. Officialdom had finally succeeded in placing Pia behind bars.

What no one had bargained for was the old man's affability. It seemed everyone liked him. The *Arizona Daily Star* rallied to his defense, and even McKinney, the arresting officer, took the side of the Native Americans. Their efforts, however, were futile. Pia was tried, convicted, and sent to prison.

But the story does not end there. The old man who had rebelled against the white man's ways was enchanted by the jail's indoor plumbing, central heating, and electric lights. They were comforts he adapted to with enthusiasm. He found much to admire about the food and made a lifelong friend of the jailhouse cook. Guards were so captivated by the old Papago's charm, they led him on clandestine sightseeing excursions through the city and, it is said, took him on an airplane ride.

After serving eighteen months in a variety of federal prisons—and finding something to his liking about each—Pia returned to the reservation a different man. He insisted that the children attend the white man's school and encouraged his male followers to register for the draft. Arizona's last Native American uprising had been quelled. Pia had been assimilated.

Chapter 6

Circles in the Desert

"NOUVEAU CRIMINALS" MAY BE an apt description of Irene Schroeder and Glenn Dague. They made headlines for a brief time and shortened their lives by making them. In an era of glorified gangsterism, neither achieved glory, but each would be remembered—at least in local circles—for a number of uncomfortable days given to Arizona lawmen.

Irene, described by the Associated Press as "stolid and unromantic in appearance," was a twenty-one-year-old waitress from Wheeling, West Virginia, and the mother of a four-year-old son, Donnie, whose father had left them. Glenn was a Wheeling automobile salesman who taught Sunday school and was the father of two children and the husband of a schoolteacher. He was described as "pale-eyed and dapper."

Something—it is not known what—drew the two together in an illicit love affair and a brief career in banditry. Two days after Christmas 1929, Irene and Glenn held up a grocery store in Pennsylvania. A pair of highway patrolmen, Brady Paul and Ernest Moore, pursued them. On a road near Newcastle, Paul was shot dead, Moore wounded. The lovers fled west.

East of El Paso, Texas, the duo picked up a hitchhiker, a man calling himself Joe Wells. The duo became a trio and headed toward the Pacific coast. Wells, a two-time Oklahoma ex-convict whose real name was Vernon Ackerman, was no stranger to illegal activity. Together, the three pulled a holdup in El Paso, then continued their westward trek.

On the afternoon of January 13, 1930, seventeen days after the murder in Pennsylvania, a cream-colored Chrysler convertible came to a stop at a filling station in Florence, Arizona. A large blonde, the sole passenger in the vehicle, emerged from behind the wheel and told the owner she was en route to her mother's deathbed in Yuma. She was out of gas. Could he spare a few gallons? She would certainly repay him. Caught by her ruse, the man pumped some gas into the stolen auto's tank.

The woman then drove to another station. This time the story was a sick child in Yuma. Could she possibly be given ten dollars and a few gallons of gasoline in exchange for a good spare tire? This attendant was less gullible and sent her on her way.

She drove to a third station, but unbeknownst to her, off-duty sheriff's deputy Joe Chapman was right behind her. Finding her activity questionable, his policeman's curiosity peaked. Before she could engage the attendant in conversation, Chapman approached and asked to see the Chrysler's title. The young woman's nervous fingers made cursory movements through her handbag, but no title was forthcoming. All at once, she laced her arms about the steering wheel and pushed her body into the horn. Its loud blasts brought her two accomplices scurrying from across the street to the filling station. Suddenly, the woman produced a gun, one of her cohorts did the same, and Chapman—unarmed and defenseless—became the unwitting captive of an unemployed waitress and her Sunday-school-teacher boyfriend.

With Glenn behind the wheel, Irene in the rumble seat, and Wells' revolver fixed in Chapman's ribs, the quartet sped into the desert in what

Downtown Florence where the Schroeder-Dague odyssey began.

Deputy Joe Chapman, who led his captors in circles around the desert.

would be an odyssey of rain, mud, dust, and bullets. Chapman's life would be spared, he was told, only if he led his abductors over a safe route to California. If he failed, he would die.

Chapman, his wits very much intact, conjured up the notion of leading his captors over a wide circle in the desert and keeping them within the boundaries of Pinal County. Confident that he would be rescued but acutely aware of the risk a police shoot-out posed to his own safety, he wanted officers present who were familiar with his face.

Meantime, the sheriff was on the long-distance telephone line with his counterparts in the central and southern parts of the state, requesting of each that roadblocks be thrown up in their jurisdictions. A posse of Florence citizens was organized, and small groups were dispatched to watch various junctions and bridges and to patrol side roads. No one knew the identity of the trio, but it was assumed they were desperate and dangerous.

Chapman led the party past the Feliz Farms, through the Gila River bottom, and across the main highway between Florence and Coolidge. There they purchased gas at the Bell Boy Service Station—with money stolen from the deputy's pocket—then were off again on rutted, muddy roads.

Twice, the vehicle broke down, and the lawman was forced to dig out the wheels, but Chapman had succeeded admirably in confusing their sense of direction. The trio of crooks had no idea where they were going—no idea it was nowhere. Then Glenn, impatient with the delays, insisted that Chapman take them on a more reliable road west. Having no alternative, the captive deputy reluctantly led them into Maricopa County.

Rain splattered the windshield as the Chrysler convertible sped toward Chandler. White knuckles probably gripped the steering wheel when Glenn saw the headlights of an oncoming car, but after a moment, the car passed without incident and disappeared into the night. Its passengers, the Pinal County sheriff, his deputy, and the Florence town marshal, had not recognized the cream-colored automobile they sought.

Four men stationed at the southern edge of Chandler were not so easily fooled. Officers Lee Wright, Shirley Butterfield, Joe Smith, and a night watchman named Lindly saw the approach of the speeding convertible. Unable to stop it, Butterfield and Wright jumped into Butterfield's car and took after the Chrysler in hot pursuit. Near the town plaza, Butterfield overtook the stolen vehicle, surged in front of it, and screeched to a halt at a forty-five-degree angle. The fleeing automobile was stopped dead in its tracks.

Wright got out of the passenger door, shotgun in hand, and was met by a hail of gunfire from the Chrysler. Blinded by the car's headlights, all he could do was level his weapon in the direction of the fire, pull the trigger, and hope for the best. It did not produce the desired effect. Deputy Chapman's hand was shattered and the side of his head skinned by the blast. Dazed but recognizing that it was then or never, Chapman kicked open the door and literally fell from the automobile. He picked himself up and stumbled across the curb—then his worst fears were realized. Thinking he was one of the kidnappers, the officers opened fire on him. Miraculously, none of the bullets made its mark before he was able to throw his hands in the air and scream, "I'm Chapman! I'm Chapman!"

Lee Wright was not so fortunate. One of the bandit's bullets caught him in the shoulder and knocked him to the pavement. A vein was severed, and blood gushed. He would live only a few days.

Seizing the moment, Glenn quickly put the Chrysler in gear, backed away from Butterfield's vehicle, and sped down the road in a cloud of dust. Experienced lawmen had been foiled by amateurs. The hunt began anew.

A long, agonizing vigil followed. Every available patrol car in Maricopa County was brought into the search, but it was not until two-thirty in the morning that a substantial lead developed. It was then that a Phoenix radio station flashed the news that a cream-colored Chrysler convertible had been discovered abandoned about a mile and a half beyond the Indian agency on the Maricopa reservation. Glenn, Irene, and their tagalong had made a mistake.

Officers converged on the scene and quickly concluded that the trio of fugitives had fled on foot toward the Gila River bottom, where they could hide until first light. Through the night and into the morning, lawmen tracked footprints leading to the desolate Estrella Mountains. Just before noon, an airplane was deployed to the area, and soon the trio was spotted huddled in a depression. Eight deputy sheriffs were directed to their hiding place. The moment they came into view, a barrage of hostile fire whipped the air. It then became obvious that a contingent of lawmen would have to come in from behind.

Leon Sundust, a Native American of the Maricopa reservation who knew the terrain well, gathered together a few of his tribesmen and led the way. All at once, the desperate trio found itself surrounded by heavily armed and deadly serious men. Irene was the first to surrender. "Don't shoot," she pleaded, thrusting her hands into the air and stepping into the open. Glenn and Joe followed her lead.

The prisoners were handcuffed, placed on horseback, and led down the slope of the mountain and back over the trail on which they had come. The nouveau criminals' brief career in banditry had concluded.

Back in Pennsylvania, little Donnie Schroeder, going on five years old, was quite impressed by his mother's notoriety. "She shot two cops," he would tell anyone willing to listen. Of course, he did not comprehend the statement's implications, nor did he understand why his mother did not come to visit him.

The last he remembered was his mother taking him to his grandfather's house and kissing him good-bye. Donnie did not know she had been fleeing from a holdup and murder and going west. Later, the police came and took him to a juvenile home, where they gave him a big rabbit. With the furry white creature cuddled in his lap, Donnie—unwittingly—made good fodder for insensitive photojournalists. Irene had made her son a momentary celebrity.

The boy did not know that during his mother's brief moment of celebrity, the press—always seeking a creative moniker—had dubbed her the "Blond Bandit" and the "Trigger Woman."

Charged with first-degree murder in the death of officer Lee Wright, Vernon Ackerman, a.k.a. Joe Wells, was tried, convicted and sentenced to life in prison. However, it would be a short sentence. On October 20, 1931, he dropped dead of a heart attack in his cell at Florence.

Irene Schroeder and Glenn Dague were extradited to Pennsylvania, where they stood trial in the death of highway patrolman Brady Paul. Each was convicted. Each was sentenced to death.

"Mrs. Schroeder's face was pale, almost ghastly, except for a slight bit of rouge on either cheek," reported the Associated Press as Irene was led to the death chamber at Rockview Penitentiary at Bellefonte, Pennsylvania, February 23, 1931. "Her eyes were open until she was seated in the big chair, then she closed them and kept them closed until the death hood was placed over her head."

The AP report went on to say that Glenn "came in with a steady stride and as he sat down in the chair, gazed left and right at the witnesses. Then the hood was adjusted, and the electric contact was made while the prison chaplain was still offering up a prayer for the condemned."

Irene Schroeder gained the dubious distinction of being the first woman electrocuted in the state of Pennsylvania. It is not known if Glenn Dague was the first Sunday school teacher to meet such a fate.

Chapter 7

Arizona's Last Lynching

"WHETHER AN EFFORT WOULD be made to prosecute any of the fifty or more men who participated early yesterday in the lynching of Starr Daley for killing James Ray Gibson and attacking Mrs. Gibson on the Apache Trail Thursday night remained undetermined today when Governor Thomas E. Campbell declined to discuss the lynching."

That ambiguous sentence appeared as the lead item beneath a splash of headlines on the front page of the May 7, 1917, issue of the *Tucson Citizen* four days after Daley, a young drifter from Oklahoma, had turned a patch of desert beneath the Superstition Mountains into a killing ground.

Gibson, described as a "stocky, well-knit man," was a thirty-four-year-old traveling salesman for Hitchcock and Hill, a Chicago grocery wholesaler. He and his attractive thirty-six-year-old wife, Florence, had visited his parents in Globe, then pointed their Dodge touring car toward the couple's Tucson home. They were driving the old Apache Trail, a rutted dirt road that catapulted out of the mountains in a series of switchbacks and curves. Sensible people did not drive Arizona's primitive roads at night, and as dusk approached, the Gibsons made camp near Weeks' Station, some twenty-four miles east of Mesa. They had learned from experience that motoring in Arizona's desert country demanded preparation and always traveled with camping gear and provisions.

Darkness had settled over the camp when a young man wearing dust-laden western garb strolled out of the brush, a weary saddle horse trailing behind him. He asked for and was given a drink of water. Then, in a moment's flash, the stillness of the night was broken by the report of a .32

caliber rifle, its deadly force directed at James Gibson. There are conflicting accounts regarding the number of shots fired. One says three, another four. According to the *Arizona Republican*, Gibson's body was riddled by six bullets, the last two fired at point-blank range into the man's skull as he lay dying. What is certain is that each round fired was from the rifle of a cold-blooded killer.

With Gibson's body lying in a pool of its own blood, Daley turned his attention to Florence. Reporting in the breathless style of the day, one newspaper wrote, "She spent the whole of Thursday night on the Apache Trail with her husband's murderer, her clothes taken from her and under the threat of death, subjected to every whim his seemingly degenerate mind could think of."

Mercifully, daylight came. Florence was forced to cook breakfast and pack the car while Daley, using the dead man's razor, shaved off his mustache in an attempt to disguise his appearance. In later testimony at a coroner's jury, Florence quoted Daley as telling her, "We will leave the body here and forget it, then get married, sell the car and go to Oklahoma." The notion of entering a marital union with her husband's killer must indeed have been a chilling one to Florence.

Keeping strained wits in check, she agreed to his ridiculous proposal but told him he would have to kill her before she would abandon her husband's body in the desert. If Daley wanted to marry her, he must agree to transport Gibson's body to a mortuary in Mesa that could effectuate a decent burial. The young killer acquiesced.

The body was wrapped in a blanket, lugged onto the back seat of the Dodge touring car, and covered over with camping equipment. With Daley behind the wheel and the terrified Mrs. Gibson at his side, the unlikely couple started off toward Mesa.

A fortuitous turn of events occurred on East Main Street at the outskirts of what was then a small Mormon farming community. The automobile ran out of gas. And that is when Daley made the mistake that would ultimately cost him his life.

He did not force Florence to accompany him but left her in the car with her husband's body and set out alone, on foot, in search of a filling station. It was about six-forty-five in the morning, and Mesa was quiet, but after a few moments, H. S. Phelps, a local resident en route to work, came by on a bicycle. Florence flagged him down and, near hysterics, told him of her plight. Phelps rushed to the home of city marshal Tom Peyton, interrupted the lawman's breakfast, and relayed Florence's story. Peyton leaped to his feet, strapped on his .45, and grabbed a shotgun and thrust it into Phelps' hands. The two men dashed from the house and headed toward Main Street. Daley was in clear view, pouring gasoline from a can into the vehicle's tank.

The arrest was simple and without incident; the killer offered no resistance. Florence was given over to the care of a physician; Daley had a preliminary hearing in the justice court at Mesa, then was bound over to Maricopa County sheriff W. H. Wilky and put behind bars in the county jail in Phoenix. Newspapers across the state headlined the grisly murder and the heinous assault of the victim's wife. Emotions ran at a feverish pitch, and good men and women from all quarters of society cried out for justice. Daley was a marked man.

The murderer had no hesitation in admitting his crime—to authorities and newspaper reporters alike. "I was a fool to take the body in the car," he is quoted as saying. "Anyway, I read the papers. I know they can't hang me. And I know no jail can hold me for long."

And therein lay the rub. Regardless of the beastly nature of his crime, the most severe punishment the state could mete out was life in prison. Just five years had passed since the granting of statehood, and Arizona voters reasoned that the state's six-shooter image could be countervailed by eliminating the gallows. They did this in 1916 by a margin of 152 votes out of 37,720 cast. Daley would cause them to agonize over that decision.

Talk of vigilante action buzzed about the streets of Phoenix. This was a crime so depraved that a prison sentence—even life in prison—seemed a mere slap on the wrist. Justice must be done.

"At midnight five hundred or more men—and not a few women—visited the county jail in quest of the murderer," reported the *Tucson Citizen*. "Men had been gathered in knots about the streets all evening talking of a lynching bee, but it was midnight before they advanced on the jail itself."

Sheriff Wilky, aware of the agitation fulminating in the streets of the capital city and cognizant of his sworn duty to protect his prisoner's life, set upon a course of action to prevent mob violence. At this juncture, conflicting accounts come into play. The most likely scenario, however, is that Wilky, having explained the seriousness of the situation to Daley, enlisted the killer's cooperation in a ruse that was intended to fool the crowd outside the jail and provide safe transfer of the prisoner to the penitentiary at Florence—out of reach of the Phoenix belligerents.

The account states that the unshackled Daley and deputies Sam Barrett and Charles Musgrove "strolled from the courthouse, shouldered their way through the crowd, and approached an official car." Confident they had duped the jailhouse onlookers, the trio took off on Adams Street at high speed, wanting to put as much distance as possible between them and the agitators before their ploy was discovered.

After the deputies and their prisoner had sped away, reported the *Tucson Citizen*, Wilky "allowed the leaders [of the mob] to look into all the cells to see for themselves that Daley was not there. Since no one in the crowd had ever seen the prisoner . . . even if Daley had been there it would not have done much good so long as he was able to bluff it out."

The story goes on to say that "it was a most orderly crowd so far as outward evidences went. There was no display of pocket artillery, but there was no doubt but that the leaders were there for business if they found the man they wanted. However, the real leaders were far away speeding after the flying car of the sheriff which was, even as the crowd approached the jail, passing through Mesa bound for Florence."

The ruse had failed. Within minutes, according to one account, several dozen automobiles were on both roads leading to Florence in hasty pursuit of the deputies and their prisoner. One of the pursuers called ahead, and a blockade of cars was set up at the bridge near the Florence depot. When almost within spitting distance of the prison, deputies Barrett and Musgrove were stopped dead in their tracks by a contingent of angry citizens determined to take the law into their own hands. The deputies made a quick turnabout and headed in the direction whence they had come, but it was a futile effort. They were overtaken again and forced to stop their flight. Five men emerged from the chase vehicle and approached the lawmen.

The *Tucson Citizen* took up the story: "Not a word was said. In the meantime, the other cars, attracted by the stationary lights, came up making a circle around the captured car, with all lights glaring in the faces of the two officers and their prisoner. A spokesman was selected, and leaving his gun behind, he advanced to the parley. Everyone wore a white handkerchief around his face, and it was impossible to identify any of the vigilantes."

Given the obviousness of the situation, the question was almost rhetorical; nonetheless, the deputies asked what the men wanted.

"We want Daley."

When the deputies replied that they could not give up their prisoner, two armed and masked men stepped up to the vehicle, opened the door and motioned for Daley to get out. Surrounded by an armed mob, there was nothing more the deputies could do. They turned their vehicle around and headed back to Phoenix to alert authorities about what was happening.

Daley was on their turf now, and the vigilantes told him that if he tried to bolt he was a dead man. He made assurances that he would not but asked that he be permitted to make a statement. His captors granted the request.

"I want you all to understand that my mother made me what I am," he was quoted by the *Tucson Citizen* as saying. "She brought me up to do her bidding. She ran a brothel when I was young and she used to make me go out and seduce girls and bring them in to work there. I killed Gibson and I did what I wanted with his wife."

The vigilantes calmly informed Daley that he would be returned to the scene of his crime and hanged. He accepted his fate stoically and agreed to lead the way, talking freely as the motorcade proceeded into the desert. He told his captors that he had been raised near Bartlesville, Oklahoma, by his mother and stepfather—a known bank robber—and that his real name was Van Ashmore. He boasted of bank robberies he had participated in with his stepfather and said he was certain he had killed a couple of men along the way. The most bizarre of his revelations was the story of a little brother who had been removed from the family by the state and placed in a foster home. The mother and stepfather located the boy and, to retaliate against the state, murdered the lad by pouring boiling water over him. The story was never confirmed, and authorities were quick to point out that Daley was a "creative liar."

"Now I tell you, gentlemen," the *Citizen* quoted Daley, "I know I am guilty, but I think the people who brought me up, my mother and step-father, are more to blame than I am. I don't know where they are, but I hope they hear of this and that someone punishes them too." He concluded by saying, "I am willing to be hanged, but I hope you won't burn me or shoot me full of holes."

He was assured that his body would not be mutilated, and the procession of vehicles continued to its destination, Daley chain-smoking the entire journey. He badly wanted a drink, but each time he asked, he was told there was no liquor in the automobile and that the crowd was "dry."

At last, they arrived at their destination. The lead car stopped near a telegraph pole, and the other vehicles pulled into a circle around it. By now, the group had swelled considerably. Some reports say more than one hundred people were present. Most put the number at about fifty, including two women said to be taking a "lively interest" in the spectacle.

Apparently, Daley had more expertise in tying a noose than did the vigilantes. The *New York Times* reported that "he showed the mob leaders how he wanted the noose to be adjusted and urged that he be hanged so his neck would break rather than to be strangled to death."

The same article says Daley was given an opportunity to pray. "He could only murmur, 'Oh my God.' With heads bared in the moonlight, while Daley knelt, every man repeated the words of the Lord's Prayer."

A long, white rope was tossed over the crossbar of the telegraph pole; one end was tied to a mesquite stump. "Let's do it right," Daley is purported to have said. "Back a machine up here, and let it be pulled out from under me."

An open car was brought around, and the condemned man was hoisted onto the backseat. The noose was put about his neck, and at Daley's request, his hat was placed on his head. Asked if he wanted to make a final statement, he replied that he did and again absolved himself of guilt by placing blame on his mother. "I hope this will be a lesson to all men like me. I am not to blame. It is the result of having a mother who worked in a brothel."

An anonymous foot stepped on the throttle of the car, and the automobile surged forward. "And then the perpetrator of the most sensational crime in the history of Arizona was swung into eternity," said the *New York Times*. But in reality, Daley did not find eternity so swift in coming.

"He got what lot's of other people ought to get," was inscribed on the back of this 1917 photo of Daley, lynched at the scene of his crime.

After a few moments, someone in the crowd asked, "Is he dead?" A doctor stepped forward, felt the killer's wrist and listened for a heartbeat. "He will be in about two minutes," came the reply.

Some fifteen minutes later, the vigilantes dispersed, and Daley was left alone, dangling from a telegraph pole as the dawn of a new morning looked down on the desert.

What no one would know until later is that Governor Thomas E. Campbell had spent hours racing in his automobile about Pinal County in an effort to locate the lynch mob and intercede in its vigilante justice. It was a wasted effort. The governor's night could better have been spent in bed.

The *Citizen* of May 7, 1917, reported that "a coroner's jury yesterday returned a verdict of 'justifiable homicide at the hands of parties unknown,' at the inquest on the body of Daley, which was buried in the sands of the desert at the place of execution. . . .

"The identity of none of the members of the mob was known to the officers," stated the article. "The authorities further expressed doubt that a conviction could be had even if any of the members of the mob were brought to trial."

Starr Daley undoubtedly was a creative liar. But could it be that Arizona's lawmen, judges, and politicians were equally creative? From the moment of Daley's kidnapping at Florence to the moment of his lynching, every word muttered by him was reported the very next day in breathless detail—thousands of words—by newspapers across the nation. Where did the newspapers get those words? Whom were they quoting? Someone—perhaps several—among the vigilantes had much to say and said it with gusto to a press most willing to listen. And yet, state authorities were unable to identify a single member of the group responsible for Daley's hanging. Indeed a curious situation.

The next year—1918—by a vote of 20,443 to 10,602, capital punishment was restored in Arizona. A brutal murder at the foot of the Superstition Mountains had not been forgotten.

Chapter 8

The Disappearance of Aimee Semple McPherson

"I CAN'T STAND the jingle of coins," she once told her adoring congregation when complaining about frayed nerves. "Make it a silent offering. I can't hear paper money."

Called the only woman alive whose first name alone was sufficient to carry a headline on the front page of any North American newspaper, Aimee Semple McPherson entered the world as Aimee Elizabeth Kennedy in 1890 on a small farm—chronically mortgaged—near Ingersoll, Ontario, Canada. Her mother, a formidable woman named Minnie, was a tambourine-thumping Salvation Army follower who steeped her daughter in the rigidity of fundamentalist Protestantism.

During her youth, Darwinism and the temptations of the secular world crept into Aimee's life, and her heretofore unquestioned faith in the Almighty was shaken at its core. But under the stern tutelage of a Pentacostal preacher, Robert Semple, the young girl was born again. Aimee renounced dime novels, ragtime music, and cheek-to-cheek dancing and accepted Semple's proposal of marriage. Soon bride and groom were off to China as missionaries.

Within a year, Semple dropped dead of dysentery, and Aimee found herself on the sidewalks of Manhattan, broke and with a baby to care for. In quick succession, the resourceful eighteen-year-old widow married Harold McPherson and by him had another child.

But marriage and children would take a backseat to the Lord. On a momentous evening, Aimee was visited by the Holy Ghost, who told her to go out into the world and spread the word of God. And that is what she did. She abandoned McPherson and took to the tent and sawdust circuit as a traveling evangelist. "The mistress of hallelujah revivalism" is how the *London Daily Mail* characterized her.

For several years, she traveled the Atlantic seaboard with her mother and children in tow, sharpening her evangelistic skills and developing a style uniquely her own. Blessed with a silver tongue and remarkable physical assets, Aimee was able to expand her following quickly, but the buxom beauty yearned for other pastures.

In 1918, with one hundred dollars in her purse and a rattletrap automobile, Aimee and family set out for Los Angeles—a town reputed to contain more eccentrics per square mile than any other city in America.

However, Aimee's first taste of genuine success occurred not in tinsel town but in San Diego, where some thirty thousand people attended an open-air revival meeting sponsored by area churches. During the service, a paralytic woman abandoned her wheelchair and staggered to the podium. As Aimee prayed for her, other ailing congregates came forward. It was the turning point of the young evangelist's career. Word spread quickly about her ability as a faith healer, and fame and fortune rapidly followed.

By the mid-1920s, Aimee had risen from obscurity to build a multi-million-dollar religious empire. Angelus Temple, an enormous circular structure, was built in the Echo Park neighborhood of Los Angeles at a cost exceeding one million dollars. Outfitted with a powerful radio station—KSFG—the fifty-three-hundred-seat auditorium was crowned with an illuminated rotating cross that could be seen for fifty miles.

Assets that served Aimee well were a flair for the dramatic and an innate ability to generate publicity. What she dubbed the "Four Square Gospel" (the FSG in her radio station's call letters) gained worldwide followers, and capacity audiences filled Angelus Temple.

A McPherson church service was no ordinary revival meeting but an extravaganza filled with music, pageantry, and—perhaps most importantly—sex appeal. While salvation was her message, Aimee, not the Almighty, was the central attraction.

She was thirty-six years old and riding the crest of fame and glory when on May 18, 1926, newspapers around the world cried out the headline, "Aimee Semple McPherson Reported Dead."

Thus began an odyssey unique in American history.

Aimee Semple McPherson.

Emma Schaeffer, the evangelist's private secretary, told police in tearful detail that she and Aimee had gone into the surf together at Santa Monica. "Mrs. McPherson went into the water ahead of her companion," chronicled the Associated Press, "who noticed she was having difficulty standing against the breakers. Miss Schaeffer said her attention was directed away from Mrs. McPherson for a few minutes and when she again looked for her the woman had disappeared."

The news was astonishing. Aimee, known to be a good swimmer, had walked into the water and, in a matter of moments, simply disappeared—presumably swallowed up in the bowels of the Pacific Ocean.

"Reports of Mrs. McPherson's dying were quick to reach members of her congregation," continued the story, "and hundreds of the evangelist's followers flocked to the beach and tonight were frantically pacing the shore.... All available police have been dispatched to the beach to keep the crowd under control."

While scores of Aimee's flock hunted the beaches of Santa Monica

Bay, scanning each breaking wave in the hope that the ocean would cough up their leader, an airplane circled above searching the water and all available lifeguards were dispatched to the scene to comb the beach and probe the surf.

The next day plans were made to explode depth bombs in an effort to surface the body. It was reasoned that ocean currents would carry a body southward along the bay toward Redondo Beach, several miles distant, and the search was focused in that direction. A Coast Guard cutter was sent out, deep sea divers employed, and grappling hooks put into play.

As the search for Aimee's body continued, supporters gathered day and night around Angelus Temple, chanting, "Aimee is with Jesus. Pray for her." Mother Kennedy, reported the press, was "firmly in the belief that the evangelist had been drowned."

But two days after the evangelist's disappearance, the story took on a startling new complexion when a Culver City detective insisted that he had seen Aimee in the company of another woman in an automobile bound for Los Angeles at the very time she was reported missing.

The AP hinted at things sinister: "A theory of possible violence, centering about the evangelist's opposition to the election measure, recently carried, permitting resumption of Sunday dancing at Venice.... [An] underworld character . . . [is] said to have openly threatened Mrs. McPherson following her alleged declaration that she would rather see her children in their graves than in a Venice dance hall."

One of Aimee's followers, a man "overcome by emotion and . . . [a] long watch on the beach" declared he saw the image of the pastor walking on the water. Police discounted the report.

Aimee had been gone eight days when the AP reported that a "new and thorough investigation of the disappearance" would be undertaken. "This investigation, authorities indicated, would be along lines contrary to the accepted theory of her thousands of followers and others that the Angelus Temple pastor was accidentally drowned...."

The next day, Los Angeles district attorney Asa Keyes announced that if the evangelist's body was not discovered within twenty-four hours, he would begin a "vigorous investigation of the case and . . . would seek for questioning Kenneth G. Ormiston, formerly radio operator at Mrs. McPherson's temple and one of her close friends."

It was the first mention of Ormiston, who in 1923 had installed KFSG and operated the station until the previous January, when he himself had disappeared. Ormiston's wife Ruth had filed a missing persons report.

Ormiston's mother, who lived in San Francisco, volunteered that her son had separated from his wife "following a quarrel over Mrs. McPherson." The wife had filed divorce papers, then returned to her family home in Australia.

"Ruth was always jealous of Mrs. McPherson," said the mother, "but I don't believe there was any foundation for her jealousy. My son had the deepest respect for Mrs. McPherson, but he and his wife quarreled over her a number of times. The disagreement finally broke up the family."

Ormiston reappeared long enough to meet secretly with Mother Kennedy on the beach at Santa Monica and to be questioned by police. He admitted that his wife was divorcing him and naming Aimee as corespondent but disclaimed any connection with the evangelist's disappearance. He added that he was confident Aimee had been drowned and that her body would wash up soon.

That said, Ormiston disappeared again.

On May 28 a Venice police captain swore in an affidavit that he had been at the beach at the exact spot and time when Aimee allegedly disappeared and that "no person, man or woman, was swimming there."

It was a pointed contradiction of Emma Schaeffer's story and served to fuel speculation and innuendo. The press removed its gloves, tongues slipped into cheeks, and skepticism replaced eulogies.

Mother Kennedy, in a move that many saw as a contradiction of her stated belief that Aimee was dead, offered a twenty-five-thousand-dollar reward for her daughter's safe return. Coincidentally, the same day she received what the police deduced was a crank ransom note. "Send fifty thousand dollars and she is yours," read the disjointed missive. The note instructed her to place the money on a westbound streetcar at a specific time. "We'll deliver her within half an hour after pay. Mum's the word. Keep police away."

The instructions were not followed, and nothing further was heard from the would-be kidnappers.

"While an airplane strewed white and crimson roses over the gentle swells of Santa Monica Bay," wrote the AP on May 30, "thousands of [Aimee's] followers crowded today into Angelus Temple . . . to conduct a memorial service."

Actually, three services—morning, midday, and evening—were held, throngs of mourners jamming the temple's aisles at each. And it did not go unnoticed that thirty-six thousand dollars went into the collection plate, ostensibly to complete a Bible school as a memorial to the fallen evangelist.

Meantime, the Los Angeles Police Department reiterated its belief that Aimee had drowned but to cover its tracks, it proffered theories that the evangelist might have absented herself for private reasons, that she might be the captive of kidnappers, or that she might be the victim of amnesia or murder.

Three days later, Captain Herman Cline, chief of detectives for the LAPD, took charge of the investigation, stating that "the prominence [of Aimee] and the recurrence of reports that she was not dead demanded a careful sifting of all evidence in the public interest." Cline then left for San Francisco in search of Kenneth Ormiston.

The following day, the *Sacramento Bee* reported that three residents of Biggs, a small town in Butte County, north of the capital city, had witnessed Aimee and a male companion taking breakfast in a local cafe. It would be one of hundreds of Aimee sightings across the country.

Seventeen days after the evangelist's disappearance, Mother Kennedy announced that the search of Santa Monica Bay, carried on by church members, would be discontinued. "We have endeavored amid all the billows that have surged around [us] . . . to face the situation with Christian fortitude and common sense," she told the press.

After three fruitless days scouring San Francisco for Ormiston, Detective Cline returned to Los Angeles empty-handed and told the press he believed Aimee had drowned as reported. This summation, however, would not be Cline's last word about the case.

Insisting that she had never wavered in her belief that Aimee had gone to her maker, Mother Kennedy nonetheless renewed the twenty-five-thousand-dollar reward for her daughter's safe return. The reward, which was to have expired at midnight, was extended until midnight of June 12. For many, it seemed an odd thing for Minnie to do.

Some 450 miles over the mountains and across the desert, in Tucson, Arizona, Aimee was the subject of a June 7 editorial. "Nearly three weeks have elapsed since the disappearance of Aimee … while swimming on the beach at Santa Monica," wrote the *Arizona Daily Star*, "and yet the public interest in the case will not run down. Few stories have had so long a 'run' as has this one. … No matter how important may be the other news of the day, the first question on the lips of most readers when they unfold their paper is, 'Is Aimee found yet?'"

The *Star* had no way of knowing that it and other Arizona newspapers would come to play an important role in the story of Aimee's disappearance.

As the investigation continued, three additional memorial services to mourn the evangelist's death were held at Angelus Temple. Afterward, Mother Kennedy petitioned Los Angeles County for an official death certificate. The county coroner refused, declaring there was no evidence that Aimee was dead and expressing his personal belief that she was alive.

And she was very much alive.

"Resurrected from 'Dead' Aimee Safe," began a bold splash of startling headlines on the June 24 issue of the *Arizona Daily Star*. "Kidnapped from Beach; Evangelist Held for Ransom; Staggers to Border; Relates Lurid Story of Adventure and Cruelty."

In a story datelined Douglas, Arizona, *Star* reporter Gilbert Cosulich—a man with a penchant for billowy prose and a loose regard for fact—wrote, "With chloroform, gags and thongs as part of the 'properties,' a harrowing tale of abduction by automobile and an escape after a twenty-mile delirious wandering in the Mexican desert, was told tonight … by Mrs. Aimee Semple McPherson."

But Cosulich, apparently captivated by the buxom evangelist, was more interested in describing Aimee than he was in relating the "harrowing tale." "From time to time, as she spoke, she would raise a well-rounded white arm to smooth her luxurious brown hair. … Clad in a becoming pink crepe de chine robe de chambre, Mrs. McPherson sat propped up in bed in the west wing of the hospital. … Her room was filled with gladioli and other flowers sent by the chamber of commerce, several of the churches, and others.... Outside the hospital hundreds gathered on the street to catch a glimpse of the famous evangelist."

Just after midnight on June 23, Frederick Schansel, German-born custodian of a slaughterhouse that straddled the international border a mile east of Agua Prieta, Sonora, Mexico, and Douglas, Arizona, was awakened by his dogs' barking. Clad in his underwear, he went into the yard to quiet them and found a woman leaning against his gate. When asked what she wanted, she replied that she wanted the police. "What you done?" probed Schansel. She said she had done nothing but had been the victim of kidnappers. The woman did not volunteer her name but asked him if he had a telephone. He did not. Did he own an automobile? He did not. She then asked if there was a woman in the house. When he replied in the negative, she asked how far it was to a house with a telephone where there would be a woman. Told it was about a mile, the woman started off at a brisk pace toward the indicated designation.

Smitten by curiosity, Schansel dressed hurriedly and followed her to Agua Prieta, then returned home scratching his head. He concluded that she was an eccentric American bent on circumventing prohibition.

Ramon Gonzales, proprietor of the O.K. Bar in Agua Prieta, had just gotten into bed when he heard a woman's voice shouting, "Hello! Hello!" He answered the call and was asked if he had a telephone. When he said he did not, the woman asked where she could find a telephone to call the police. Concerned, Ramon and his wife, Theresa, left the house but did not immediately see the woman. Then they saw a body lying by the gate. Fearing she was dead, Ramon rushed across the street to the home of Ernesto Boubion, *presidente* (mayor) of Agua Prieta. Discovering he was not at home, Ramon dashed back to the gate, lifted the woman in his arms, and carried her to his porch. Placing a pillow beneath her head and covering her body with a blanket, Theresa noticed that the woman's hair rested neatly in a silk hairnet.

When at last the stranger revived, she began to speak rapidly. The Gonzales', who spoke little English, understood little of what she said. Just then Boubion returned home and Ramon summoned him. The *presidente* listened to the woman, who was still speaking rapidly, and decided an interpreter was needed. Leaving the stranger in Theresa's care, he and Ramon drove into town, picking up Police Chief Sylvana Villa on the way, and soon returned with Johnny Anderson, an American who operated a taxi between the two border towns.

When Anderson spoke to her in English, she "clung to him as if he were her only hope." She told him she was Aimee Semple McPherson, that she had been snatched by kidnappers five weeks earlier, had managed an escape about noon the previous day, and had since been wandering in the desert. Anderson translated her story to his Mexican companions, and Boubion instructed him to take the woman in his taxi across the border to the police station in Douglas.

It was just before four A.M. when the taxi pulled up at police headquarters. It was quickly decided that Aimee—if indeed the woman was Aimee—should be taken to the hospital. In the company of officers George W. Cook and O. E. Patterson, Anderson drove her to the Calumet and Arizona Hospital. Aimee was not, however, given a cheerful welcome. The attending physician refused to admit her unless she was able to prove she could pay for hospitalization. While each man was skeptical about her identity, Cook magnanimously obligated himself to pay the woman's bill should she prove indigent. Aimee was admitted.

Once inside a private room, Aimee was undressed by a nurse, who noted red marks on her wrists and two small blisters on her toes. Otherwise the evangelist was in astonishingly good condition for one claiming to have wandered hours on end over rugged desert terrain. She was not dehydrated, emaciated, or even sunburned. Her lips were not cracked or swollen. Her temperature, pulse, and respiration were normal.

One of the officers notified the police chief, then telephoned the Douglas and Bisbee newspapers. Before the dawn of a new day, the chief, a sergeant, and William McCafferty, editor of the *Douglas Daily Dispatch*, were at the woman's bedside. McCafferty had met Aimee in Denver and swore that she was the missing evangelist. The policemen examined her shoes and clothing, which—despite sensational press reports to the contrary—were in remarkably good condition, then asked Aimee to recount her story.

She told of going to the beach at Santa Monica with Emma Schaeffer but contradicted Schaeffer's report that the secretary had joined her in the water:

> I thought of some details concerning our meeting and I asked Miss Schaeffer to attend to them.... While she was away I decided to take a dip, and walked into the water, waist deep.
>
> Suddenly I heard my name called by someone on the beach. I was annoyed at being disturbed. I saw a woman and a man standing on the beach. They began crying, and told me that their baby was dying and they wanted me to pray for it. The woman ran on ahead, after having given me a long coat to wear, which she had conveniently at hand.
>
> "Hurry," the woman said, "or my baby will die."
>
> The woman had been holding what seemed to be a baby, but it turned out to be a bundle of clothing, which she capped over me and made me smell something which I later found to be chloroform.
>
> This happened at two o'clock in the afternoon, as nearly as I could judge. It was dawn of the next day when I awoke in bed. The room was in a house that I believe was in Mexicali or somewhere near San Diego, from what I could catch of the conversation by the people around me.
>
> I felt very sick at the stomach. Three persons were in the same house. One was a woman they called Rose, who had black hair, dark brown eyes, full lips and weighed about 185 or 190 pounds and who seemed to have been a nurse.
>
> One of the men was called Steve. He was rather heavy set, but not fat, smooth shaven, with brown hair, and he wore a brown suit.
>
> The other man's name I did not hear. He was tall and dark, was flat chested, had sparse hair and a gold tooth.
>
> They told me that they wanted $500,000 ransom for me. When I told them that I did not have that much they answered, "Pshaw, you have got millions."
>
> I was in that room all the time, up to about four days ago. Then they moved me in the same auto to another place during the night, and we reached our destination the next morning.

This time I was placed in a room that was very meagerly furnished. There were two cots, one for Rose and the other for me. The men slept in another part of the house, and their conduct towards me was respectful, except that one of them burned one of my fingers with a cigar while trying to get some information.

About four days ago Rose told me she had to go away to get supplies and said she would have to bind and gag me. "You don't mind Dearie," she always called me Dearie, "for after Friday everything will be all right, if your mother does the right thing."

I had noticed a can in one corner of the room. It looked like a varnish can. I knew that if I could get to it I could cut off the flat bands with which Rose had tied me by using the sharp edge of the can's lid.

I rolled off the cot, and cut off the strands that bound me. I was nearly wild with joy when I found that I was succeeding, and I gave thanks to God for giving me strength to do it.

I ran out into the desert. I suppose I wandered about for twenty miles during that afternoon and evening. It was terribly hot and I had no water. I ran gasping and feverish among the cactus and got considerably scratched up.

Finally I struck a road, and ran along the highway for about eight miles. At about nine-thirty that night I came to the outskirts of a town and heard dogs barking and a man swearing at a dog.

Over the months, the story would be embellished upon and altered here and there to suit the occasion, but that essentially is what Aimee asked the world to believe. Never mind that her attending nurse did not find her parched from lack of water, feverish, or "considerably scratched up."

Mother Kennedy boarded the train for Douglas, the AP reported. So did District Attorney Asa Keyes and Detective Herman Cline. "How was a woman like Mrs. McPherson, known almost all over the civilized world, kidnapped in broad daylight on a crowded beach?" Keyes asked rhetorically. "Why was a twenty-five-thousand-dollar reward offered for her safe return withdrawn, then re-offered and withdrawn again June 12?"

Curiously, after Aimee's resurrection, Emma Schaeffer was forbidden by Mother Kennedy from talking to the press. "No, you must not see her," Minnie told reporters. "She is nervous and she can't talk very well. She just isn't that sort, you know. She doesn't know [anything]."

"The secretary," wrote the AP, "attired in black, and her eyes red from weeping, was a pathetic figure amid the excitement at Angelus Temple."

Could it be that Schaeffer's pathos was the result of knowing too much and the fear of her involvement in a cover-up?

After countless press reports describing Aimee's disheveled appearance upon entering the Douglas hospital, the sheriff of Cochise County, disgusted by the reports, told the *Bisbee Review* that neither the clothing nor the shoes worn by Aimee during her desert odyssey were damaged in any way. The items were then locked away in a local bank vault.

The next day, Mother Kennedy arrived in Douglas on the Golden State Limited and, before visiting her daughter, treated the townspeople to an impromptu revival meeting. While Douglas residents mugged for the cameras, a "moving-picture machine," mounted on the back of a truck, recorded the event for posterity.

"Plump, genial and ingratiating, the little woman's improvised services were an undeniable success," wrote *Star* reporter Cosulich, who failed to mention that only then did Mother Kennedy enter the hospital for the reunion with Aimee.

"Aimee was wearing a becoming blue silk negligee over the pink crepe de chine robe in which she had slept," gushed the reporter in a style akin to that of a public-relations writer. "Mother Kennedy rushed to her daughter's bedside, and the two women were clasped in a long embrace.

"Then the battery of photographers reappeared in the room, and six or seven flashlight pictures were taken, filling the small room with smoke."

The small city of Douglas was inundated by a crush of reporters, photographers, and motion-picture cameramen, each vying for Aimee's attention. At a soda fountain, a sign went up bearing the notation that "Aimee Sundaes" could be purchased for thirty-five cents, and at another a drink called an "Aimee" could be had for a nickel. Taxi driver Johnny Anderson approached potential customers by asking, "Do you care to ride in the seat that Aimee Semple McPherson rode in?" A reporter wrote, "All in all, it is the biggest thing that ever happened to Douglas." But a soda jerk was cynical: "The stuff that the newspapers are printing about Aimee is all bunk."

Meantime, as thousands of followers crowded into Angelus Temple to rejoice in Aimee's reemergence, Los Angeles mayor George E. Cryer told friends of the evangelist that he saw no reason why the official courtesy of the city should not be extended Aimee on her return and expressed the personal wish to meet her at the station.

As trackers scoured the Mexican desert in search of the elusive shack from which Aimee claimed to have escaped, Mother Kennedy secured her daughter's release from the hospital, and the family took a suite at the Gadsden Hotel. Hospital authorities were not disappointed when the throng of reporters and spectators moved off its property to take up their vigil elsewhere.

An editorial in the June 25 issue of the *Star* raised questions found annoying by Aimee: "Why were the shoes and clothes of the evangelist not more torn and travel-worn after her experiences? How could a woman, exhausted from wandering twenty miles in the heat of a Mexican desert continue talking to newspaper men throughout [the] day, submit to being photographed with all the local potentates, without becoming doubly exhausted and thus injuring her own health?"

One among a myriad of rumors to surface was that Aimee had gone to Agua Prieta for an abortion. But there was no foundation to the story. After the birth of her second and last child, the evangelist had undergone a "female" operation, which rendered such a notion absurd.

While McCafferty's *Dispatch* embraced Aimee's every word and offered reportage unblushingly biased, the out-of-town press was not so kind. A Los Angeles reporter asked Ramon Gonzales if he believed her story. "I do not wish to say anything against the lady," he replied, "but I think the lady is a liar."

Asked about the shack in the desert, Pedro Demandivo, chief of the Mexican border patrol—which had searched for three days—said, "[My] men know every foot of ground within fifty miles and none of them know such a cabin. If one did exist we would know about it within two days after it was built."

Unruffled, the redoubtable Aimee offered a five-hundred-dollar

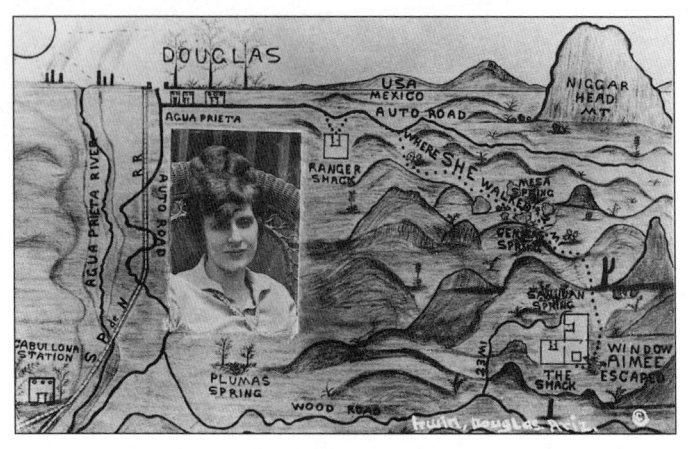

*Map drawn by Aimee showing her escape route and the shack in which
she claimed to have been held by kidnappers.*

reward to anyone who located the shack. The *Los Angeles Examiner* added
one thousand dollars and offered an additional ten thousand dollars for the
kidnappers.

When Aimee's party made preparations to leave Douglas, the Southern
Pacific Railroad offered red-carpet treatment. Eight detectives were put at
the preacher's disposal, and a special car was made available.

Having stated repeatedly the debt of gratitude she felt for the kindness
extended by the citizens of Douglas, Aimee agreed to conduct a "giant community service" at the Tenth Street Park, which was bedecked for the
occasion with American flags and red, white, and blue bunting.

At about four-thirty P.M., a band began regaling the audience with the
pomp and circumstance of military marches. At five, an automobile
brought Aimee and her family to the park. A choir representing every
church in Douglas sang two hymns. This was followed by a laudatory
address from the mayor. It was then Aimee's turn. Addressing a crowd estimated at five thousand—the largest gathering ever assembled in Douglas—
the evangelist held forth for all of ten minutes, then retired to her seat on
the platform. Given her notoriety for long-winded oration, the modest
duration of her sermon was in itself remarkable. The "giant community
service" was over almost before it began.

When the crowd surged forward to shake the hand of the famous evangelist, Aimee balked. She was whisked to her auto by railroad detectives and driven to the hotel to await her departure time.

At 9:13 the train left Douglas en route to Tucson, but before it reached its destination, reporters were scribbling out copy to let the world know that "the stage and screen ... [have] beckoned to the woman who has spent the better part of her mature years in the pulpit. From Hollywood came an offer to film the story of her life, and from a Los Angeles owner of a well-known vaudeville circuit came an offer to make appearances ... to tell of her experiences since her abduction."

Aimee refused to entertain either proposition.

Late the next afternoon, the train steamed into Union Station and, after an absence of thirty-eight days, the beloved pastor was back in Los Angeles. "Praise the Lord," she told a welcoming crowd of some five thousand. "I have suffered much, but praise the Lord I'm back with you once more."

The International News Service noted that "as she descended from her train ... a thick carpet of roses was strewn in her path and hundreds of persons cried out exclamations of happiness at the return of their leader who had been mourned for dead."

Mayor Cryer was conspicuously absent.

On the afternoon of June 27, seventy-five hundred people crowded into the fifty-three-hundred-seat Angelus Temple, where they heard their spiritual hero place her troubles at the devil's door. Relating how she had taken a stand against dance halls, the drug ring, alcohol, and the teaching of evolution, Aimee explained away her kidnapping by saying, "And so ... [the devil] finally said: 'If I could just get hold of Sister McPherson, if I could just get her away ... [the Four Square Gospel] would crumble.'"

But District Attorney Asa Keyes and Chief of Detectives Herman Cline were more concerned about the veracity of Aimee's story than they were about the devil's alleged participation, and the kidnapping investigation continued.

When reporters noted the extent of public skepticism surrounding her alleged abduction, Aimee lashed back, saying, "The sword which should be turned against the criminals has been turned against me."

When queried about rumors hinting that the supposed kidnapping might have been a ploy to cover up a tryst between lovers, Aimee spat back,

"In love with whom? Isn't it remarkable that, with all the investigation and hullaballoo that has been made, the name of the man, if there was one, has never entered the case."

On June 29 the press was told that the "joint investigation by police and the district attorney's office [had] failed to produce a single clue to substantiate the evangelist's version of her strange disappearance." That said, the AP announced that Aimee was preparing to "strike back legally at those who have cast blackening insinuations upon her story. The evangelist said two libel suits, each seeking $200,000 damages, were being drawn up by her attorneys. She would not divulge who she would name in the suits."

A day later, Aimee made public a letter purportedly received from Rose, the female member of the alleged kidnapping trio. "Dear Mrs. McPherson," it read. "Just a line to let you know I have no hard feelings about you getting away from me. In fact, I am glad it is all over with. If you could only forgive me for the part I played in this unlucky adventure I would be satisfied. But will you. Oh, please do."

The letter went on to say that Rose had "lost" her share of the money, that Steve and Jake (the first mention of the second man by name) had almost killed her and had covered their tracks and fled to El Paso.

It was an intriguing missive but one that made little sense. How had Rose "lost" her share of the money when no money changed hands between the supposed abductors and the McPherson organization?

While the LAPD intensified its investigation, trackers from both sides of the border continued to search the Mexican desert for the elusive shack in which Aimee insisted she had been held prisoner. On one day alone, eight shacks dotting a large geographical area were searched to no avail. For a few days, Aimee joined the search. Again headlines were made at Douglas, but the shack she described remained a mystery.

Ernesto Boubion, *presidente* of Agua Prieta, issued a statement asserting that Aimee's claim of being held captive in a Sonoran Desert shack was pure fabrication. Boubion said he believed that the evangelist, instead of tramping miles across the desert after escaping from kidnappers, had in reality been driven from Douglas to a shack four miles east of Agua Prieta, then brought even closer to town, from which point she had staggered into the border community.

The preacher refused to discuss the statement, but Mother Kennedy shot back, "That's Mexico, Mexico," implying that Boubion's ethnicity precluded him from making sensible judgments.

The same day as Boubion's report, it was learned that a grand jury had indeed been called to investigate the case.

Then, on July 5, it was announced that "new and startling information" had been brought to light, that the LAPD wanted very much to chat with Kenneth B. Ormiston, Aimee's former radio operator, who himself had disappeared.

Twenty-four hours later, District Attorney Keyes laid the entire matter before the grand jury, issuing subpoenas for Aimee, daughter Roberta, Mother Kennedy, and an assortment of Angelus Temple workers. Requests also were forwarded to Douglas and Agua Prieta asking officials to come to Los Angeles to testify.

A new wrinkle developed when, on July 7, Tucson automobile dealer O. E. Pape identified a photograph of Aimee as a woman he had seen in Agua Prieta three days prior to her reappearance. Volunteering to testify before the Los Angeles grand jury, Pape told the *Tucson Citizen* that Aimee was "the smaller of two women whom he had seen at the International Cafe at Agua Prieta." Pape said the women were in the company of two men and one of the men "closely resembled a picture of a Los Angeles man who is said formerly to have been connected with Angelus Temple."

Aimee laughed it off. "Isn't it ridiculous that anybody should say they had seen me coming out of a roadhouse?"

When the evangelist arrived at the hall of justice on July 9 for her first appearance before the grand jury, it was show time in typical Aimee fashion. As reporters' flashbulbs popped, two lines of Angelus Temple workers, robed in blue and white and each carrying a hymnbook, formed a pathway through which their leader entered the hall.

In the lobby, a man dressed in clerical garb sold printed tickets purporting to entitle the holders to seats in the grand jury room—never mind that the hearing was conducted behind closed doors. Some two dozen people bought the worthless tickets at two dollars each before the man was arrested.

The press was unable to quote what Aimee told the grand jury but did report that it was probably the smallest, least responsive audience the evangelist had ever addressed.

It was learned the following day that District Attorney Keyes had received a telegram from *Presidente* Ernesto Boubion stating that the Mexican official had new information to the effect that a large blue automobile had been parked near Niggerhead Mountain, a well-known peak near the border, on June 22, the day before Aimee made her appearance in Agua Prieta. Several persons asserted that they had seen the same automobile at different points about the border carrying, among other persons, a woman closely resembling the evangelist.

Boubion claimed that the automobile had taken Aimee to a ranger shack, where she got out and intentionally made footprints around the structure. That done, she had returned to the car and was driven to a point near the slaughterhouse on the road to Agua Prieta, where she encountered Frederick Schansel, the German-born custodian, and later Ramon Gonzales and his wife.

Meantime, interest in Ormiston was increasing, and on July 11, a subpoena was issued ordering him to appear before the grand jury. The only problem, however, was that no one had a clue as to where Ormiston was.

"Mrs. Minnie Kennedy, unheralded, unguarded and unattended, today appeared before the Los Angeles County grand jury," wrote the AP on July 13. The appearance, which lasted about an hour, was said to have focused on the financial affairs of Angelus Temple prior to Aimee's disappearance.

Ormiston was in the headlines again July 16, when a garage owner in Salinas identified Aimee and him as a couple who had patronized his establishment on May 29, eleven days after the evangelist's disappearance.

"After Ormiston's car had left Salinas," wrote the AP, "it was reported to have been traced to San Luis Obispo where its driver and a woman registered at a hotel as Mr. and Mrs. Frank Gibson, later driving south to be accosted by a newspaper man at Santa Barbara, where the driver denied he was Ormiston."

Mother Kennedy responded with typical indignation: "The fires of hell are burning and they must burn themselves out, but we are not afraid."

And the search for Ormiston continued.

Much to Aimee's satisfaction, the grand jury ruled on July 20 that the evidence presented was insufficient to warrant an indictment against her. District Attorney Keyes, however, said that his office would not consider its investigation closed until it had an opportunity to question Ormiston. Aimee's attorneys, quite naturally, were delighted with the grand jury's decision and issued a statement that said, "The official investigation not only bears out her story and proves it true, but reveals her to the world as a truthful, upright woman, who has withstood the attacks in a religious, God-fearing manner."

Five days later, an explosion erupted in the press when Deputy District Attorney Joe Ryan revealed that four credible witnesses had identified Ormiston and Aimee as a couple who had rented a cottage for ten days at Carmel-by-the-Sea and that he had samples of the evangelist's handwriting as well as fingerprints.

Aimee's initial reaction was stunned silence; then, through her attorneys, it was learned that she had flatly refused to submit to a fingerprint examination and had refused to submit handwriting samples for comparison. When it was suggested by Detective Cline that Aimee go to Carmel to face the witnesses, Mother Kennedy declared that her daughter was needed too badly at the temple and had no intention of leaving Los Angeles.

Because no charges had been brought against the evangelist, the authorities' hands were tied.

More cooperative was the foreman of the grand jury, who announced that he was ready to reopen the investigation on the basis of the Carmel evidence.

After Aimee had gotten her tongue back, she declared that Cline and Ryan were making a "determined effort to dig up dirt and filth wherever they could and hurl it at me."

"I have been chosen," she continued dramatically, "the lamb for every kind of slaughter, but I won't be slaughtered either financially or morally."

The grand jury reopened its investigation July 29, and Aimee was subpoenaed to appear. Asked if the new investigation was to determine whether the evangelist had committed perjury in her previous testimony, District Attorney Keyes said yes.

Three days later, Keyes contradicted himself. "To convict Aimee ... on charges of perjury would cost the county thousands of dollars. It takes conclusive evidence in a perjury case and I feel that the evidence Cline and Ryan have received at Carmel is too vague to successfully prosecute anyone on a perjury charge."

The grand jury was not happy about Keyes' statement and ordered the district attorney to continue his investigation.

On August 23 a woman calling herself Lorraine Wiseman appeared at the office of Aimee's attorney with the claim that she was the sister of the woman who had stayed with Ormiston at the Carmel cottage and that she had been there with them. She then produced an affidavit signed "Miss X," which purportedly had been written by her sister.

"I have been unable to sleep since this thing happened," said Wiseman. "Although I know ... [it] ... may ruin my name, I can't stand by and see another woman suffer for an indiscretion in which she was not connected in any way."

Then, just as it appeared that Aimee might be vindicated of the Carmel accusation, the strange woman was arrested and jailed on bad-check charges. She proclaimed her innocence, however, insisting a twin sister was the guilty party.

There was no twin sister, and the woman's name was actually Lorraine Wiseman McDonald Sielaff. Nor was there a "Miss X." Setting off a bombshell that reverberated in the bowels of Angelus Temple, Sielaff stated emphatically that Aimee had paid her five thousand dollars to lie on her behalf. "It was a pure premeditated hoax born at Angelus Temple and launched from that source on glib and golden promises," she told police. "Mrs. McPherson and her mother at various times gave me money to use for expenses in framing the hoax. They were always free with cash."

"The whole thing is a pack of lies," countered a furious Aimee. "Anything [she] has said at the county jail, she has found in her own imagination and there is no truth to it."

In an astonishing turnabout, Aimee admitted the next day that temple funds had been given Sielaff to conduct an "investigation" of the alleged Carmel incident. "Of course we forwarded Mrs. Wiseman-Sielaff funds with which to carry on her investigation," said the evangelist. "We did so just as we did with detectives and others who believed they could obtain evidence in clearing up my case."

On the heels of this new development, District Attorney Keyes said he and his aides "had discussed the question of whether the arrest of the evangelist should be ordered, and determined that . . . [a] decision on this move rested on further investigation."

"It's martyrdom," sputtered Mother Kennedy. "We have known for weeks that they have planned to drag Sister McPherson from the pulpit of Angelus Temple in a sensational arrest."

Then on September 16, the AP broke the news that "[the] arrest of Aimee Semple McPherson . . . Mrs. Minnie Kennedy . . . Kenneth G. Ormiston . . . John Doe . . . and Mrs. Lorraine Wiseman-Sielaff was ordered late today by District Attorney Asa Keyes." Formal complaints were drawn up charging the five with conspiracy to defeat justice.

Counsel for Angelus Temple immediately informed the district attorney that Aimee and her mother would be surrendered as soon as the warrant for their arrest was prepared and served.

In timely fashion, however, Aimee collapsed during morning services at the temple, telling the congregation she was too ill to continue. Later, her physician issued a statement saying that "Mrs. McPherson is suffering from one of the most dangerous infections I know of, which is abscess of the nose close to her brain. There is very, very great danger that it may go to her brain. Death, I fear, would follow."

Whether or not the illness was a ploy, it worked. The next day, Mother Kennedy was arrested on a charge of criminal conspiracy and released on twenty-five hundred dollars bail after being in the custody of the district attorney for forty minutes. Minnie pleaded not guilty.

According to the AP, "[The] formal arrest of Aimee . . . was deferred owing to her physical condition and probably will not physically take place."

Four days later, after a miraculous recovery, her congregation cheered as Aimee once again took up the pulpit at Angelus Temple, announcing that she was launching a "fight the devil" fund. She asked her followers to dip into their pockets to the tune of at least one hundred dollars a head.

Although she was not physically arrested, bond was posted, and on September 28, a preliminary hearing on charges of criminal conspiracy began. Before the day was over, six witnesses testified that they had seen Aimee in the company of Ormiston at the Carmel cottage.

The hearing was six days old when Aimee's flock gathered at the temple to witness "The March of the Martyrs," an elaborate tableau portraying famous biblical scenes and depicting the "history of persecution."

A parade of witnesses, including many from Douglas and Agua Prieta, told their stories, and on November 14, after weeks of explosive testimony in one of the longest preliminary hearings on record, Aimee was bound over for trial on criminal conspiracy charges. Also charged were Mother Kennedy and Lorraine Sielaff. "After a full examination of the entire evidence," ruled the judge, "there is sufficient cause to believe the defendants guilty."

The AP wrote that "the evangelist went white as she heard the decision that sent her to the superior court for trial on the charges that she conspired to manufacture evidence supporting her story of kidnapping ... and to refute the allegation that she spent ten days in a Carmel cottage with her former wireless operator, Kenneth G. Ormiston, fugitive co-defendant."

At last, on December 9, Kenneth Ormiston was apprehended at Harrisburg, Pennsylvania, where he had been living for two months under an alias. Returned to California on December 18, he was taken into custody by the LAPD and charged with criminal conspiracy. Two days later, he was back on the streets under twenty-five hundred dollars bail pending his arraignment.

In an odd twist of irony, Lorraine Sielaff, the catalyst for the charges brought against Aimee and the others, would prove to be their unwitting savior. It seems the woman found it impossible to tell the same story the same way twice. In essence, she was a habitual liar unable to separate truth from fiction.

"The McPherson case is now in such a muddled state that a conviction is almost impossible and the charges probably will be withdrawn," District Attorney Keyes told the press on December 29. He cited as the reason "the collapse of the testimony of the principal witness," Lorraine Sielaff, whom the district attorney characterized as a "turncoat" and a "perjurer," saying she had told a "different story every day."

As muddled as the case may have been, Keyes' contradictory statements were not adding clarity. "A bewildered public, vainly attempting to follow the intricate case, was further puzzled tonight by a statement by District Attorney Asa Keyes emphatically denying that the case against Mrs. McPherson…will be dropped," penned the AP the very next day.

Keyes' statement read, "Emphatically, I will not drop this case. While [Sielaff] has changed her original story in part, it is not diametrically opposite to what she told on the witness stand during Mrs. McPherson's preliminary hearing. Instead, it is more of an elaboration of the vague parts of her previous testimony."

While the public tried to make sense of Keyes' vacillation, the *Los Angeles Times* received a cable from Sydney, Australia, quoting Ruth Ormiston, Kenneth's estranged wife, as saying she had received a "most impertinent" letter from Aimee—mailed to her on May 18, the day of the evangelist's disappearance.

While refusing to disclose the contents of the letter, Mrs. Ormiston said it was her intention to use it in divorce proceedings, which she intended to institute in Los Angeles after the first of the year.

On New Year's Day 1927, Kenneth Ormiston testified before the Los Angeles grand jury, tracing his movements from the day of Aimee's disappearance to the day he was apprehended, all the while insisting that he was in no way connected to Aimee's disappearance. He admitted that he had spent ten days at the Carmel cottage but insisted that his companion was a nurse from Seattle—not the evangelist.

On January 6, at the penitentiary in McAlester, Oklahoma, Coleman Rickerson, a twenty-four-year-old lifer, came out of the woodwork to announce that in 1924 he had been approached in Casper, Wyoming, by two men from Montreal who sought his participation in a scheme to collect two million dollars in a series of kidnappings. The first victim would be Aimee, followed by Hollywood stars Mary Pickford and Jackie Coogan and other names not so famous but known to be connected to large sums of money.

It was an interesting tale but just one of hundreds told since the unfolding of Aimee's drama.

Meantime, as the evangelist awaited trial, she announced that "whatever the status of [my] case may be," she would leave the following week on a speaking tour of the United States.

Then, on January 10, Keyes again startled the public by reversing his position. It would be the last time.

"The case against Aimee ... who was recently held for trial on criminal conspiracy charges, today was transferred on request of the county's chief prosecutor from the law courts of California to the court of public opinion," reported the AP.

"Superior [Court] Judge Albert Lee Stephens, on motion of District Attorney Asa Keyes, dismissed all the charges against the evangelist, her mother ... Kenneth G. Ormiston ... and Mrs. Lorraine Sielaff, growing out of prolonged investigation of the mysterious disappearance and reappearance of the picturesque pastor last spring and her kidnapping story told in explaining her absence.

"In asking the dismissal, however, Keyes did not vindicate the Four Square Gospel leader of charges that she left here last May 18, not in the hands of kidnappers, but in the automobile of Ormiston bound for a cottage at Carmel, California. He reiterated the state's contention that Mrs. McPherson had perpetrated a hoax but declared that he could no longer proceed on the often changed stories told by Mrs. Sielaff, the evangelist's chief accuser."

But for the cheering at Angelus Temple, it was all over. The case against Aimee was closed.

In a scathing editorial, the *San Diego Herald* wrote, "The failure—or perhaps the innate inability—of some women to keep their legs crossed has been the cause of more wars, murders and general crimes than all the other reasons in the catalog ... and as a modern lesson to a modern world it has made Aimee Semple McPherson out to be the most chuckleheaded liar that ever dallied with her Lothario in a bungalow by the sea or tasted the delights of forbidden love in a cottage just big enough for a folding bed that never folded, and a stove that at its best was a good deal cooler than the flaming desires of those who giggled beside it in the dark."

A magazine called the *Haldeman-Julius Monthly* wrote that "while Aimee's followers had roamed the beach ... searching for her body, several of whom caught visions of her rising from the waves and ascending to Heaven, the reverend 'Sister' was alive and pulsating, had been a dweller in the Garden of Aphrodite; that when airplanes were scattering flowers over her watery 'grave,' the lady was devoting herself to the shrine of Venus."

In the years that followed, Aimee established more than four hundred branches of her Four Square Gospel and sponsored missions around the world—but her life was never the same.

Discord erupted at Angelus Temple over financial policies. In a violent argument between mother and daughter, Aimee broke Minnie's nose, and an estrangement followed. Roberta, Aimee's daughter and heir apparent, was involved in a lawsuit against her mother, and another estrangement followed. And the ensuing years saw countless lawsuits filed by disgruntled followers and temple workers—lawsuits that would haunt the evangelist the rest of her days.

But the redoubtable Aimee rolled along, pausing just long enough to partake of the latest Paris fashions or to undergo an occasional face-lift—and the money kept pouring in.

The public was stunned when on September 27, 1944, Aimee died of an overdose of barbiturates. Fifty thousand mourners passed by her coffin as the body lay in state at Angelus Temple, the evangelist's hands clasped over an open Bible.

Whether her death was by design or accident is still a mystery. But an even greater mystery taken to the grave with Aimee was her whereabouts for thirty-four days during the spring of 1926.

Chapter 9

Arizona's Last Train Robbery

IT MUST HAVE SEEMED like a splendid idea—affixing a mask in old West fashion over one's nose, strapping on a shooting iron, and blowing open the safe of the Rock Island Golden State Limited. It would be a piece of cake, for the element of surprise surely would be on the yeggs' side. After all, some thirty-five years had gone by since anyone had been bold—or stupid—enough to attempt a train robbery in southern Arizona.

A rather ordinary lot, the principals did not possess characteristics typical of Hollywood's glamorous bandits. Tom Dugat, chief schemer, was an unpleasant man with financial difficulties who ran a goat ranch in the desert southwest of Tucson. His lieutenant, George Winkler Sr., owned a clothes-cleaning establishment in town and was thought to be a respectable citizen. His sons, Edward and George Jr., were likable enough fellows who did their father's bidding. Frank Jirou, who cared for an ailing daughter and was down on his luck, was a restaurant man who had once cooked barbecue on West Congress Street. And Santiago Valdez was an immigrant goatherd in Dugat's employ and a relative stranger to the others.

By 1922 much had been forgotten about train-robbing etiquette; thus the unlikely desperadoes scorned the discomfort of saddle leather and rode to the rendezvous in Winkler's six-cylinder Nash touring car. Getting to their destination, however, was one of the very few things that went according to plan.

During April, five of the six (George Jr. was too young to be considered useful) met on at least three occasions at the Dugat goat ranch. There they drank freely of unlawful liquor, became intoxicated, watched Dugat casually boil broken sticks of dynamite in a kettle over the stove to make nitroglycerine, and elaborated plans to divest the Golden State Limited's express car of its contents.

Given their lack of experience in such matters, the men concocted a rather sophisticated plan. A patch of desert a mile and a half south of Jaynes Station, a tiny farming community some nine miles northwest of Tucson at milepost 977.4 on the Southern Pacific tracks, was selected because of its distance and obscurity. Dugat and his cronies clocked the train from the Tucson depot and knew to the second how long it would take to arrive at the destination they had chosen. Torpedoes and fuses would be used in a standard configuration to bring the train to an emergency stop. Then orders would be given the train crew to uncouple the express car. Placing putty about the cracks of the safe to subdue noise from the explosion, they would blow open its door and collect the riches. It would be a simple, tidy operation.

Or so the thinking went. What they had not figured into the equation was Harry Stewart, an obstinate express messenger who was handy with a firearm.

It was just after nine o'clock on the evening of May 15, 1922. George Winkler Sr. and his elder son, Edward, were about to leave for Jaynes Station when George Jr., a teenager possessed of healthy hormones, created a complication he would later regret. "My brother ... came to us ... because he had made a date and wanted ... [the] car," twenty-two-year-old Edward would later testify. Told that it was out of the question, the youngster then insisted on tagging along wherever Edward and his father were going. Against Edward's better judgment, the father acquiesced. Here was a man untroubled at the prospect of making criminals of his progeny—or of the danger involved.

At about nine-thirty, Edward related, "We called on Jirou ... [then] went out along the Silverbell Road ... [where] we picked up Tom Dugat and the Mexican...." At a crossing near Dugat's ranch, they transferred gunnysacks of firearms and explosives from the goat rancher's pickup truck to the Nash, and it was there that Edward prevailed over his father and forced George Jr. from the car, "telling him that we were going to holdup the Golden State and that he could not come any further."

Abandoned in the dark of night, ostensibly to guard Dugat's empty truck and with unsettling knowledge of what his brother and father were about to attempt, George Jr. probably would rather have been on his date.

Sometime later, the party arrived at its destination and parked well away from the tracks where the automobile was hidden by a clump of mesquite bushes. With time on their hands, they built a fire against the late-night chill and prepared for the train's arrival. Dugat presented George Sr. with an automatic rifle and gave Jirou a .44 caliber revolver. Edward owned a gun he had purchased sometime earlier at a Meyer Avenue pawn shop. Then George Sr., who had been employed for a time as a railroad fireman, enlisted Edward's assistance in positioning the torpedoes and fuses along the tracks. At 12:40 A.M., the Golden State Limited, running a few minutes behind schedule, came into sight.

According to the rules of railroading, the first two torpedoes were a sign to slow down, the third a signal to come to a complete stop. Not one to argue with regulations, engineer George L. Reid halted the train at almost the exact spot designated by the bandits.

"No sooner had he stopped," an *Arizona Daily Star* reporter would write, "than a man [Dugat] wearing a mask came from the side of the right of way and climbing up the steps of the engine cab ordered him [Reid] to put up his hands. He testified that the masked man giving the order brandished a revolver, and that he did as ordered. Another masked man [Jirou] . . . came up from the left side of the engine and covered the fireman [Maurice F. Ingham] with the revolver. Then both men were ordered from the train."

"In the meantime," recounted the engineer, "the bandits had found Charles R. Bailey, . . . [who had hopped a freight car], and he was brought up to the point where the engine crew was standing." A hobo from Kentucky, the unwitting Bailey would be pressed into service.

As Edward, Jirou, and Valdez guarded the train crew and the hobo, Dugat gave George Sr. the signal to uncouple the express car from the main body of the train. And that's when the plan began to run afoul.

Despite his experience as a railroad man, George Sr. was not up to the task. Coupling equipment had been improved, and he did not know the new system's mechanisms. All at once, according to the *Star*, he turned to Bailey and "poked his gun in my face and swore, and told me to get down the train and cut off the mail and express car. Well, the way he said it, I didn't hesitate....

> So I started on down the track and got about even with the [express] car and straightened up with his hat square in my face. He poked me in the ribs with the gun and said I couldn't uncouple them from that side and that I'd better get on the other side awful quick.
>
> Believe me, I crawled under that car right now and I came out on the other side so fast that I nearly knocked another of them off his feet. Then he started poking me with the gun and told me to make the uncoupling awful speedy. By that time it was getting wild so when I got between the cars I crawled underneath and started running along under the car. The fellow with the glasses on [Dugat] shot at me three times, and I could hear the bullets sing all around me.

The terrified hobo ran the entire length of the train, dodging about beneath the cars, and on reaching the end, continued down the track as fast as he could until he was out of sight.

"Bailey's experiences were nerve-wracking to the highest degree," wrote the *Star*, "but nevertheless contain what is probably the one humorous element in the affair. It is Bailey's first trip west, and he says that it surpasses his wildest dreams of the 'wild and woolly' West."

Meantime, the express car still needed to be uncoupled or the evening's escapade would be for naught. George Sr., with forced assistance by the train crew, at last effected the uncoupling, then ordered the engineer to pull the train forward. Told there was not sufficient steam to do so, Edward got into the act, calling the engineer a "damn liar" and telling him that he "had better start moving the train." To emphasize his point, Edward injudiciously fired three rounds from a .33 Colt revolver into the ground. It was sufficient persuasion, and Reid pulled the forward cars half a dozen car lengths up the track.

That task completed, Reid and fireman Ingham were told by Dugat and George Sr. to approach the express car and order its keeper, Harry Stewart, to open the door and come out with his hands in the air. They did, but Stewart, a gritty sort of fellow, was not so inclined and refused to comply with the order. Then the bandits themselves banged on the door and ordered Stewart out of the car. Again the tenacious express messenger refused. He had no intention of giving up property entrusted to his safe-keeping—at least not without a quarrel.

Grown impatient at the messenger's obstinacy, Dugat determined that extreme action was in order and began placing sticks of dynamite around the express-car door. If Stewart would not open the door, Dugat's dynamite would.

It was a fatal error. Before anyone had time to react, reported the *Star*, "Stewart wedged the barrel of a .45 (one account says a shotgun) through a slot in the door and blew a hole through Dugat. "I . . . heard shots from the opposite side of the train," testified Edward, who had been sitting on the ground with his back resting against a telegraph pole. "I went over to the left-hand side [of the train] and found Dugat lying on the side of the track on his back. He was moaning and I asked him what had happened, and he said in a feeble voice, 'I don't know.'"

As Dugat lay dying, an unnerved George Sr. assumed command and called in his troops, whereupon the novice holdup men fled in a panic. "After the bandits disappeared," wrote the *Star*, "[a] witness declared that he heard an automobile start up. He assumed that it was larger than a Ford because of the fact that he heard the shifting of gears."

It was an astute observation. What the witness heard was the Nash touring car—George Sr. at the wheel—start up and speed away in the direction whence it had come. After driving a short distance, he pulled to the side of the road and traded seats with Edward. His nerves were too frazzled to drive, he told his son.

Edward continued south toward the crossing near Dugat's goat ranch, where George Jr. was waiting. Sirens wailed in the night, and at St. Mary's Road, they met a speeding hearse en route to Jaynes Station to collect Dugat's body. It was a disquieting sight.

At the cutoff, Valdez left the automobile and disappeared into the brush, and George Jr. came aboard. "I became so nervous," said Edward, "that I had to turn the wheel over to my brother ... who drove Jirou home, and then we returned to our home about two A.M."

Moments after the failed bandits deserted the scene, extra freight number 2702 puffed in from the east. Alerted to the situation, conductor B. S. Montgomery backed his train into Jaynes Station and wired the chief dispatcher at Tucson, who in turn notified the sheriff's department. Twenty-five minutes after Dugat had been felled by a .45 slug, law enforcement and Southern Pacific Railroad officials converged on the scene of the bungled train robbery.

As the investigation got under way, headlines blazed across that morning's issue of the *Star.* "Despite energetic efforts made by Sheriff Ben F. Daniels and his deputies," wrote the newspaper, "as well as by officers of the Southern Pacific Railroad, to apprehend the robbers, the identity of the six or seven men who aided T. O. Dugat, Tucson goat rancher, in holding up the Rock Island Golden State Limited near Jaynes Station early Sunday morning, remained a mystery at one o'clock this morning."

Five sticks of dynamite were found at the scene, four of them by "J. W. Sinks, special officer of the Southern Pacific Railroad, who also found a sack of putty and a flashlight, all believed to have belonged to the robbers," wrote the *Star.* "A hat, also thought to have belonged to a member of the gang, was picked up by Mr. Sinks, but since the inside hatband was torn off, this article furnished little in the nature of a clue.

"The four sticks of dynamite found by Mr. Sinks were well taped up, indicating, so the officer said, that the caps and fuses had been adjusted by skilled professionals."

Hardly. But the notion made good copy. Rank amateurs had left the area strewn with evidence that would tie them to the crime, including a thermos jug of nitroglycerine (not mentioned in the initial press reports) and a generous quantity of fingerprints.

Dugat's body was taken to the morgue, fingerprinted, and positively identified almost before the dust had settled in the tracks of the Nash getaway car. It was simply a matter of time before the identity of the other culprits would be known.

"If the [six] men who were in the holdup Monday morning of the Rock Island train had seen *Turn to the Right* that is showing at the Opera House . . . there probably would have been no holdup," proclaimed Roy Drachman, promoting the silent film then playing at his familys' downtown theater.

"The moral taught and the scenes shown in this picture is without question the greatest lesson for a prevention of crime that has been shown on the screen for many a year.

"Illustrating the morbid curiosity of the crowds regarding persons who have been implicated in accidents or crimes," reported the *Star*, "it was stated yesterday by H. H. Grimshaw, one of the partners of the Parker-Grimshaw undertaking establishment, that more than one thousand persons visited the office Monday and Tuesday to ask permission to view the body of Tom Dugat.

And so it went.

Three days after the attempted holdup, a former railroad employee was arrested and charged as an accessory after the fact. It was a false arrest, and the headlines it made proved an embarrassment to the Pima County sheriff's office. Three days later, after the Southern Pacific Railroad and the American Express Company had offered a combined reward of thirty-six hundred dollars—or six hundred dollars a head—Frank Jirou was apprehended.

Locked away in a dreary cell at the Pima County jail, Jirou may have pondered the fact that, according to existing statute, anyone convicted of robbing a train carrying the U. S. mail could be sentenced to life imprisonment or given the death penalty. A week after his arrest, Jirou turned state's evidence and, in the parlance of the day, became a "songbird."

In quick order, arrest warrants were issued for George Winkler Sr., his sons, Edward and George Jr., and Santiago Valdez. Before noon the same day, both Georges were arrested, leaving Edward and Valdez still on the loose.

"Although the other two men are at large," reported the *Star*, "their whereabouts is known, and it is expected they will be arrested soon." Based on various sightings, it was "known" by authorities that Edward was in California and Valdez had fled to his native Mexico. While Valdez probably had gone south of the border, Edward was not even in close proximity to California.

"I left Tucson May 21, 1922, riding the rods of the Sunset Limited," Edward later admitted. George Jr. had seen him off at the railroad yard. He went first to El Paso, Texas, then to Kansas City, Missouri, where his brother shipped clothing to him under the name "Barthells." From Kansas

City, he backtracked to Denver, then to Omaha, Nebraska, and finally to Minneapolis, where, on May 30, according to the *Star*, he was arrested for carrying a concealed weapon, "which was the gun I took off Tom Dugat" (after he had been shot). "I was given a ninety-day suspended sentence, and a year's probation with orders from the judge to return to Tucson."

Meantime, George Jr., whose only culpability lay with his unfortunate parentage, was bound over to juvenile court, slapped on the wrist and released. George Sr., who pleaded not guilty, was given a trial date for the second week in November. The officials were hoping that by that time they would have Edward and Valdez in custody as well. Sentencing of Jirou, who had pleaded guilty, was postponed indefinitely, the intention being to sentence all of the culprits en masse.

Law-enforcement authorities offered an optimistic, if not confident, face to the press, insisting now that both Edward and Valdez were most certainly holed up at Mazatlán, Mexico. But one month rolled into the next, and no arrests were made. Then on August 1, a press report from Hutchinson, Kansas, caused a ripple of excitement.

Arthur Lang, held in the Reno City, Kansas, County jail on suspicion of bank robbery, "tallied in every respect with the printed description of Edward Winkler broadcast by the American Express Company immediately after the train holdup," stated the report. The description, supported by a photograph of the wanted man, contained full Bertillon-system measurements and fingerprints taken when Winkler was serving in the U. S. Army.

Tucsonan C. J. Huss, who had been acquainted with Edward for a number of years, was sent by the American Express Company to Hutchinson to make a positive identification. He had agreed to wire his conclusion directly to Pima County sheriff Ben Daniels. Before he had an opportunity to do so, however, Daniels received a wire from Hutchinson authorities informing him that Lang's fingerprints did not match Edward's army prints. Soon thereafter, Huss wired that Lang "bore no resemblance to the alleged holdup . . . [man]." It had been, pure and simple, a case of mistaken identity.

After the Kansas debacle, wrote the *Star*, "officials generally voiced the opinion that the place where the holdup men will eventually be found will be in Mexico. At the police station, it was stated that the clue coming from

Mazatlán, Mexico, was by far the most likely...and should not be dropped." It was not dropped, but it did not matter. Edward was not in Mexico but in New Mexico.

He longed, according to the *Star*, to "hear what was happening in Arizona; how the... [investigation of the] holdup was progressing; how his family was faring. He made up his mind he would...[go] to Phoenix, where his aunt...lived...thinking that from her he could learn how his father and mother were.

"Acting on this impulse he went to Albuquerque, New Mexico [presumably en route to Phoenix], and about Labor Day secured employment in the Santa Fe [Railroad] shops."

It would be Edward's last stop as a fugitive from justice. A Tucson man working in the shops recognized him and notified authorities. On September 18–nearly four months to the day after the train robbery–Edward was arrested by officers of the Albuquerque Police Department.

Pima County sheriff Ben Daniels, in the company of two Southern Pacific Railroad agents, rushed to Albuquerque to claim the prisoner, but not before Edward had confessed to the local constabulary. He waited for Tucson authorities, however, before admitting that he was tired of running and glad it was over.

Edward waved extradition and, closely guarded by Daniels and the railroad agents, was whisked by train to El Paso, where a later connection would be made to Tucson. Locked overnight in the county jail, he again confessed to the bungled holdup, this time implicating his father as instigator and recruiter–something he had chosen not to do at Albuquerque.

The next morning, he and his escorts boarded the Golden State Limited–the very train he had attempted to rob–for the trip home. "More than 150 curiosity seekers gathered at the Southern Pacific depot to catch a glimpse of the prisoner when he arrived here from Albuquerque," reported the *Star*.

"The young boy had what appeared to be about a five-day growth of beard," continued the newspaper. "He was well-dressed, however, wearing blue trousers with a white shirt, a stiff collar with a black, neatly tied cravat, in which was stuck a horseshoe pin ornamented with sparkling stones. Officers carried his trim, expensive-looking black bag, and two packages of laundry marked to E. F. Barthells, the name he was using when he was apprehended."

But any semblance of frivolity ended at the depot. Taken directly to the county jail, Edward was put in a cell as far away as possible from his father, to whom he would not be allowed to speak until after the trial.

The charges leveled against Edward were identical to those lodged against George Sr. At his September 23 preliminary hearing, he pleaded innocent, and bail was set at five thousand dollars. The wheels of justice were at last in motion.

"Winkler Trial Now Under Way in Pima Court," headlined the *Tucson Citizen* on November 21, the day after the jury was impaneled and indictments read against George Sr. and Edward—who were being tried jointly. Given the notoriety of the case, the trial was of surprisingly short duration.

During the next two days, a parade of witnesses passed through the courtroom as the prosecution and the defense argued back and forth. The most damaging testimony spilled from the lips of Frank Jirou, who offered every detail of the holdup plan and the subsequent faux pas at Jaynes Station. Conviction appeared a certainty, and the state would not be denied. But then, an odd twist occurred.

"George Winkler Sr. and Edward Winkler were found guilty by a superior court jury last night of participation in the attempted holdup of the Golden State Limited at Jaynes Station on the morning of May 16, 1922, and were sentenced to ten years in the penitentiary," reported the November 24 issue of the *Citizen*.

But that was not the final word. "After the reading of the verdict, the jury summoned Ben Matthews, assistant county attorney, and John Van Buskirk, the defense attorney, to the jury room and requested Van Buskirk to prepare a petition to the board of paroles and pardons asking that Edward Winkler be immediately pardoned. Every member of the jury told Van Buskirk he would sign the petition, saying they had desired to give the younger Winkler a suspended sentence but had been told by the court that it was not in their power to do so."

The jury had been unimpressed by George Sr. and was determined that the son would not be punished for the sins of the father.

"It seems to us," editorialized the *Citizen*, "that the spirit of the jury's action should be followed out in support of any movement looking to the securing of a pardon for young Winkler, and we hope that steps will be taken looking to the bringing of the matter to the attention of the state board of pardons. If possible, in view of the jury's remarkable statement made after it had returned its verdict, young Winkler should never bear the stigma of a felon's number and habiliments."

On December 9, Edward Winkler walked away from the Pima County jail a free man. But his freedom would not be the final irony in the botched holdup of the Golden State Limited.

On December 12, Frank Jirou, the state's star witness, was not given the light sentence he had anticipated as payment for his cooperation but was banished from the state of Arizona for a period of twenty-five years and ordered to leave the state within twenty-four hours. "As Jirou is now sixty-one years old," explained the *Citizen*, "the sentence is considered equivalent to banishment for life."

Never apprehended, it is possible that Santiago Valdez fishes in his old age from the tip of a pier at Mazatlán, Mexico.

Chapter 10

Philanthropic Vengeance

A DEVOUT MEMBER OF the Methodist Church, she donated generous sums of money to organizations in which she had an interest, and her interests were many and diverse. Among those who enjoyed her largess were the Yaqui Indians, the Associated Charities, and the University of Arizona. A prohibitionist and a crusader for public morals, she established the local unit of the Audubon Society and started a Greek fraternity on the university campus.

Her name was Louise Henriette Foucar Marshall, and shortly after midnight on April 27, 1931, she pumped four bullets into her husband's sleeping body. He died.

Born into a wealthy Massachusetts family, Louise had attended school in Italy and Switzerland and become proficient in several languages. Tuberculosis and a heart condition brought her west just prior to the turn of the century. Entering Denver Women's College, she pledged Phi Beta Phi and came away from the institution with a degree in modern languages. In 1899 the fledgling University of Arizona beckoned, offering her an instructorship in Latin, French, and botany. Considered an excellent teacher, in just two years she was given a professorship in ancient and modern languages. But Louise had other interests. She abandoned the faculty in 1902 to pursue a career in business—a bold step for a woman of her day.

With considerable skill, the sickly woman parlayed a forty-thousand-dollar investment into a small fortune, involving herself in commercial ventures and purchasing buildings and land throughout Tucson. The year before she killed her husband, she organized the Marshall Foundation—still

Louise Henriette Foucar Marshall, philanthropist.

flourishing today—in an effort to avoid burdensome taxes and enable her to assist the charities of her choice.

A Kansas native, Tom Marshall had worked his way through the University of Arizona by tending its gardens. Although six years younger than his teacher, Louise, the two shared much in common. The young Marshall was introspective, reserved, religious, and had an interest in birds. Those elements qualified Tom as a prospect. Louise asked him to manage a few of her properties, a courtship followed, and soon they were married.

From the beginning of their relationship, everyone knew Tom was more or less her lackey. Louise was in command, and the husband did her bidding. He was given charge of several Marshall enterprises, but the woman of the house made the decisions.

Enter Harriet Seymour, the Marshalls' live-in housekeeper. Little is known about the woman. It is known, however, that Louise alleged that Tom was having an affair with her and that Seymour was lacing Louise's food with arsenic. Louise was convinced Tom and Harriet were determined to kill her.

On the witness stand, under oath, Matty Edwards, Seymour's successor as housekeeper, quoted Louise as telling her, "I shot him. He had been living with that woman in my own house for the past three years, and he made three attempts to poison me." Those who knew Tom insisted it was poppycock, that he was a loner without friends of either sex and was devoted to his wife.

Aghast at hearing news of the shooting, Tucsonans refused to believe a philanthropist of Louise's stature could be capable of such a dastardly deed and rallied in her defense. She was in and out of jail in a matter of hours, the legal system breaking all precedents in setting her free.

Nonetheless, Louise was charged with murder. Her lawyers insisted on a change of venue, and the case came to court in Nogales, Arizona— Louise's personal maid attending to her needs during the proceedings. The court even went so far as to provide the defendant with a rocking chair as she sat on the witness stand.

The trial lasted nine days. On two occasions, Louise broke down on the stand and was afforded time to recover. A defense attorney's dream, she was the prosecution's nightmare. County Attorney Clarence Houston was convinced of her guilt. Many years later he would say, "Tom didn't do anything. It was all in her imagination."

On September 23, a verdict of not guilty was pronounced. Spectators in the courtroom erupted in cheers. It was, after all, inconceivable that a woman so attuned to the needs of those less fortunate could be a cold-blooded murderess.

But not everyone agreed with the cheering spectators or with the jury that set Louise free. The *Tucson Citizen* wrote a blistering editorial suggesting anyone could get away with murder in Pima County, and dissenting tongues would wag for years to come.

Louise attended to her philanthropies and lived another quarter century. Now and again, she would ask a trusted confident what opinion the public had about her. Each time she was told that public sentiment was on her side—that she had done the right thing by eliminating an unfaithful husband who had tried to poison her.

She lived out her life draped in black dresses, her motherly face rarely seen in public. Many young women went through the university at her bequest, some even living in her home. She never quibbled about money and doled out funds to anyone she deemed worthy of her charity.

On January 12, 1957, at ninety-two years of age, Louise died. Members of the board of directors of the Marshall Foundation attended the funeral. Six other people came.

Chapter 11

Gunplay in the Old Pueblo

AT HIGH NOON ON September 24, 1891, a doctor and a lawyer met at the southwest corner of Pennington and Church streets in downtown Tucson. Each was a remarkable man, each a pillar of his community. One of them would live to tell about the encounter; the other would not. What transpired on that late summer day would be the stuff of legends in years to come.

John C. Handy had been born on October 20, 1844, in Newark, New Jersey. In 1853, when he was but nine years old, his family moved to California. There Handy received his education, graduating from the Medical College of the Pacific, the young state's first medical school, at the tender age of nineteen. "Soon thereafter," recorded the September 29, 1891, issue of the *Arizona Daily Star*, "he was appointed surgeon in the U. S. Army at Angel Island [California], and after having served at two or more military stations in California, he was assigned to Fort Apache, Arizona, in the fall of 1867."

In 1870 Handy was assigned to Camp Thomas, and it was there that a dark side of the young doctor emerged. He and the post trader, a Mr. Huey, exchanged words in a confrontation thought to be inspired by a woman. They would be among Huey's last.

According to a contemporary account in the *Weekly Arizonian*, Handy had shot Huey when the latter "applied to him a term for the use of which many a man on the frontier has been launched into eternity." For reasons obscure, Huey lived long enough to sign a statement absolving Handy of guilt. No charges were brought against the doctor.

It is said that Handy was one of those rare white men respected by the Apaches, that he spoke their tongue and understood their customs. "The

Dr. John C. Handy abused his wife and threatened to kill her lawyer.

Apaches regard the doctor with a species of reverence because of his success in treating their diseases," reported the *Weekly Arizonian*.

There are conflicting reports, but Handy apparently settled permanently in Tucson in 1870 or 1871. In 1932, writing a memoir for the *Star*, William V. Whitmore, a physician who had known Handy well, related a story he claimed was told him before the turn of the century by Sam Hughes, one of Tucson's earliest Anglo settlers. "Dr. Handy came to Tucson primarily to place three orphan Indian girls in suitable families here," wrote Whitmore. "While he was here, Mr. Hughes became ill and Dr. Handy was summoned. Upon learning that the doctor's plans for the future were quite indefinite, Mr. Hughes asked him how much of a guarantee would be required to persuade him to remain in Tucson. Dr. Handy replied that if he had an annual income of twenty-five hundred dollars assured, he would be willing to take his chances here. Mr. Hughes did not wait to get well, but, donning his clothes, went out upon the desert. In a short time he returned with a list of more than twenty-five names of heads of families, who agreed to pay Dr. Handy one hundred dollars a year for medical services."

Whether or not the story is apocryphal will never be known, but it is known that Handy set up a flourishing practice in Tucson and gained the admiration and devotion of the community, especially among the indigents

Mary Ann Page Handy in happier times.

for whom he was given a contract to treat. He was chief physician at the newly established St. Mary's Hospital, and when the railroad came to town in 1880, he was appointed physician for the Southern Pacific.

Handy was active in a variety of organizations, including the Masons, the Knights of Pythias, and the Legion of Honor. He founded both the Pima County Medical Society and the Territorial Medical Association and was a founding member of the Society of Arizona Pioneers, forerunner of the Arizona Historical Society. In 1886 he was appointed the first chancellor of the University of Arizona but disagreed over the board's design for the school's first building and, after refusing to attend meetings, was removed from his post.

We first hear of Mary Ann Page in the July 6, 1872 edition of the *Arizona Citizen*, when, as an eleven-year-old student, she won first prizes in arithmetic and reading. She caught the doctor's eye in 1876 when she was but fifteen, and on July 17, 1878, some two months shy of her seventeenth birthday, she became Handy's wife.

Born in Lima, New York, on March 17, 1859, Francis J. Heney had also grown up in San Francisco. His family relocated to the bay city in 1863, where Heney attended public school, then worked in his father's furniture and carpet store while attending high school at night. Later, he would teach night school while attending the University of California during the day. After graduation, he migrated to Idaho, where he served as principal of a high school, but after six months, he returned to San Francisco to enroll in law school. He was admitted to the bar in 1883. A year later, poor health would force him to Arizona's drier climate. During the four years that followed, he operated a cattle business with his brother Ben and operated the Indian trading post at Fort Apache.

Arizona's bountiful sunshine proved beneficial to the young lawyer's health, and in 1889, he moved to Tucson and settled into what would become a notable legal career.

Meantime, all was not well in the Handy household. After eleven years of marriage and the birth of five children, the relationship between the doctor and his wife was a shambles. On more than one occasion, Handy's dark side had emerged, and Mary Ann suffered the brunt of his violent temper. She confided to friends that she was constantly abused, and in December of 1888, she filed for divorce—something women rarely did in those days. Talk spread throughout the town, and tongues wagged.

No sooner had Mary Ann retained the law firm of Jeffords and Franklin than rumor spread that Handy was threatening to kill the lawyers if the case went to trial. For reasons uncertain—perhaps fear for her own life— Mary Ann dropped the suit a month later and resumed her wretched existence with the doctor.

In July of the following year, Handy took his turn at a divorce suit. By that time, Mary Ann's health was in a precarious state, and she had turned to morphine, then a popular over-the-counter drug, to relieve the pain. Handy had sent the children to live with his mother in Oakland, California, and had taken to locking his wife to a bedpost in their home.

Local gossip had it that Handy was having an affair with one Pansy Smith and that Smith had divorced her husband in anticipation of the doctor's divorce. As far away as Tombstone, the *Prospector* admonished Handy for his shameful behavior, calling Mary Ann "a good, true woman and mother."

Adding to Mary Ann's dilemma was the intimidation her husband

Francis J. Heney had a remarkable career as prosecutor and judge in California.

thrust on lawyers considering her case. C. W. Wright agreed to represent her, then dropped out. Next she hired William Barnes, but he, too, developed wet feet. No one wanted to incur the doctor's violent wrath.

Finally, Frank Heney agreed to take the case. It was a fateful decision.

Brewster Cameron, clerk of the district court and a patient of Handy's, was taken to the back room of the doctor's office on several occasions and told to deliver a message to Heney: "If Frank Heney takes that case, I will kill him!" When the clerk asked why, he was told, "[Mary Ann] is a morphine fiend and a common slut. She does not deserve any . . . [representation]."

The divorce suit was in the courts more than a year, and all the while, Handy harassed Heney at every opportunity. He tried several times to run him down with his buggy, publicly called the lawyer a coward and a son of a bitch, and tried repeatedly to provoke a fight.

But Handy had misjudged the lawyer. Heney was no coward but a man of strong moral fiber and determination. While he took the doctor's threats seriously and enacted measures to safeguard his life, he continued to represent Mary Ann.

At last, the divorce was granted. Mary Ann was deemed unfit to care for her children, and Handy was awarded custody. Mary Ann was allowed to live in the house (although, earlier, she had been coerced by Handy to sign her share of the property over to the doctor's mother) and was granted thirty dollars a month in alimony.

Not satisfied by the settlement, Handy, in July 1891, sued his ex-wife for unlawful detainer of the house. Heney again represented Mary Ann. The suit was dismissed, but the resolute doctor appealed to superior court— all the while continuing his threats to kill Heney.

Then the day came.

"I am probably the only living witness of the actual shooting," wrote J. A. Rockfellow in a letter to the editor of the *Tombstone Epitaph* on November 25, 1937.

The *Epitaph* took up Rockfellow's story: "At the noon hour, I came down the courthouse steps in company of Fred Caldwell of Willcox. We walked up Pennington Street in the center of the street within perhaps sixty yards of the corner of Church Street. Then two men came together at the corner. A pistol cracked, the men grappled and fell to the ground. A deputy sheriff dashed by us toward the spot where the two were struggling for possession of the gun. Other officers were there in almost no time.

"We could hear the officers shouting to the fighters, 'Let go that gun.' One man had the handle of the gun in his hand, the other the barrel. If either man succeeded in getting possession of it, the other was doomed. By loosening the gripping fingers, the officers got the gun. Then one of the contenders jumped to his feet and ran toward the courthouse ... for the first time we all three recognized the hurrying man as Frank Heney. He did not

Handy, in doorway of his office, tried to run down Heney with his buggy.

stop but rushed into the shelter of the courthouse. We three walked up to the corner and then saw friends helping Dr. Handy to his feet. He had been shot in the abdomen."

The *Arizona Daily Star* of September 29, 1891, continued the story: "[Handy] was helped to his office scarcely a block away. There he found his office-partner, Dr. Spencer. Drs. Fenner and Green soon arrived, they to render all assistance possible. Dr. Handy was emphatic on one thing...that he would have no one touch him but Dr. Goodfellow. In accordance with his wishes, Dr. Goodfellow was summoned from Tombstone."

George E. Goodfellow had gained a considerable reputation for his success as a gunshot surgeon. This was achieved after more than a decade of experience in Tombstone treating such patients as the Earps, Doc Holliday, the Clantons, Johnny Ringo, and Bat Masterson.

A wire was sent to the surgeon, and according to the *Star*, "a conveyance...[was arranged] for him. A Tombstone livery team, at full speed around those mountain curves took him to Fairbank. There a wheezy locomotive awaited him. Goodfellow himself drove the engine with throttle wide open over the trestles and around sharp curves of that narrow gauge of track to Benson."

Goodfellow was met at Benson by a Southern Pacific engine and again took the controls. "He took those curves west of Benson...at such a rate of speed that at one time the conductor jumped up and set the brakes of the caboose, fearing a derailment."

But the lightening journey would be for naught. "The bullet," wrote the *Star*, "had entered the left side of the abdomen about two inches below the lower rib, emerging at the very extremity of the spine." It had pierced the intestine in more than a dozen places, and Handy's prognosis was grim at best.

At 10:22 P.M., Goodfellow commenced surgery. "Just as the last stitches of the operation were being taken," reported the *Star*, "Dr. Handy expired—at 1:00 A.M., September 25, 1891."

The body lay in state at the Masonic Lodge on the upper floor of the Orndorff Hotel. "People flocked there night and day," wrote the *Star*. "Mexican women by scores remained there on knees in prayer. Guards tried to keep the number within reason, but so great was the crowd that fears were entertained for the safety of the building."

Immediately after the shooting, Heney had turned himself in to the authorities. A hearing ruled that the lawyer had committed justifiable homicide in self-defense, thus no charges were brought against him.

Handy's funeral was scheduled for Sunday, September 27, at 4:30 P.M. in the Court Plaza. The body was escorted to the plaza by members of the Masonic Lodge, the Society of Arizona Pioneers, the Legion of Honor, the Knights of Pythias, and the First Battalion of the Arizona Militia.

According to the *Star*, "The streets leading to the Plaza and the Square were crowded with people. Flags on all public buildings, the Masonic Lodge, Pioneers . . . [Society] and the Southern Pacific depot were at half mast and sorrow reigned throughout the old Pueblo.

"No more touching or more worthy tribute can be paid the dead than the sorrowing tears of the lowly," wrote the *Star* in the thoroughly condescending tone common to the era. "Tottering old men, women, little children, in fact every age and class—the great mass representing the poor—pressing forward, with sorrow stamped on every face as if bereft of their best friend, for Dr. Handy was a friend to them."

Not once in the rambling *Star* article was it stated that the mourned doctor was a wife-abuser, nor was Mary Ann's name even mentioned. Neither did the doctor's death threats to Heney or Heney's name find their way into print. "Dr. Handy was shot," was the simple explanation offered for his demise.

Some details of the divorce settlement were left unresolved at Handy's death, and Mary Ann contested the will. The effort was futile. She was left nothing.

To make matters worse, she was diagnosed with cancer of the cervix, and Dr. Goodfellow, who had since moved his practice to Tucson and taken over Handy's position with the Southern Pacific Railroad, performed a hysterectomy in May 1892. Four months later, the malignancy returned. On January 28, 1893, at thirty-two years of age, Mary Ann died an agonizing death.

But even in death, Mary Ann was not allowed to rest in peace. The cemetery in which she was buried was abandoned in 1907, and vandals made sport of destroying headstones. Finally, in 1915, her sister's husband had the remains moved to Evergreen Cemetery, where they rest today under the simple inscription, "Mary Page Handy 1860–1893, A Pioneer."

Heney fared better. Twice appointed attorney general of Arizona Territory by President Grover Cleveland, he played a prominent role in the litigation of titles under which Mexican land grants in the territory were settled and argued three such cases before the U. S. Supreme Court himself.

In 1895 he returned to San Francisco, where he engaged in civil practice until 1903, when U. S. attorney general Philander C. Knox asked that he prosecute alleged land-grant frauds in Oregon. Prominent men, including a U. S. district attorney, were indicted on charges of attempting to defraud the government, and Heney drew nationwide attention.

In 1908 Heney was appointed district attorney of San Francisco and was put in charge of a series of bribery prosecutions that implicated city officials, officers of public-utility corporations, and other prominent individuals.

Some San Francisco newspapers praised Heney's reform efforts; others scorned him. His detractors, hoping to discredit him, dredged up the Tucson shooting, embellished and sensationalized it, and spread the story throughout the city. Heney was undeterred.

"In this connection," the Associated Press would write after his death, "was the most dramatic incident ever witnessed in a San Francisco courtroom."

Abe Ruef, reputed to be a thoroughly dishonest political hack, went on trial twice in 1908. During his second trial on November 13, during a five-minute recess when more than two hundred people were jammed into the courtroom, a member of Ruef's circle walked up to Heney's table, leveled a gun at the prosecutor's head, and fired. Miraculously, Heney survived, but he would live out his life deaf in the left ear.

A juror in the first Ruef trial was arrested and charged with the shooting, only to be found dead in his jail cell with a pistol lying beside him.

In 1909 Heney ran for a full term as district attorney. He lost. In 1914 he made a bid for the U. S. Senate. He lost. And in 1918, he was nominated as the Democratic candidate for governor of California. He was disqualified by a legal technicality.

Discouraged, perhaps bitter, Heney moved his law practice to Los Angeles, where, in time, he was appointed a superior court judge.

A bright spot in Heney's last years was the warm friendship he developed with John C. Handy Jr., son and namesake of the man Heney had killed in self-defense. It was, in every way, a father-son relationship, and when the judge died in the last days of October 1937, "Jack" Handy would help carry the coffin to its grave. The Los Angeles *Evening Herald Express* would capitalize on the moment with the tasteless headline, "Heney Pallbearer to Be Son of Man He Shot."

"He was a heroic man performing heroic tasks," eulogized the minister at Heney's funeral in Santa Monica. Apparently, President Franklin D. Roosevelt, who sent a message of condolence to the dead man's widow, agreed.

Chapter 12

The Strange Case of the Odoriferous Trunks

IT WAS AN INTERESTING notion—stuffing bodies into steamer trunks and shipping them over the desert to Los Angeles. There they could be dumped into the Pacific Ocean, and no one, hungry fish excepted, would ever be the wiser. Or so the reasoning went.

Agnes Anne LeRoi's corpse fit nicely into a trunk. It was Hedvig Samuelson's body that proved problematic. It was simply too bulky. But a solution was found—surgery of sorts—and Samuelson's remains were carved into compact chunks that the trunk would accommodate. Leftovers went into a small valise.

Winnie Ruth Judd—or the "Velvet Tiger," as the press was wont to call her—purchased a ticket on the Los Angeles Limited. She checked the steamer trunks as baggage but carried aboard the valise as hand luggage. The ruse might have worked had it not been for a baggage handler at Union Station in Los Angeles with a sensitive nose.

A preacher's daughter, Winnie Ruth, née McKinnell, had been born in Illinois in 1905. Her first brush with notoriety came at age seventeen, when she put a young sailor in prison for her alleged rape and impregnation. The sailor was behind bars several months before Winnie Ruth admitted she had not been raped and was not pregnant.

Another curious episode occurred the following year, when she was found in the garage of an Illinois minister. For reasons obscured by time, the young woman was clad in a gunnysack and little else.

In 1924, at age nineteen, Winnie Ruth married forty-one-year-old Dr. William C. Judd, a fat, balding, pedestrian man. Because of a drug problem— thought to be morphine abuse—the doctor suffered chronic unemployment.

In 1930 the couple relocated to Phoenix, then a dusty little city of forty-eight thousand with one distinguishing characteristic: heat. Winnie Ruth was hopeful the dry climate would keep her tuberculosis in check; her husband was hopeful of finding gainful employment.

They rented half a duplex at 2929 North Second Street and set about to find work. The young wife secured employment with the Leigh Ford family, members of the bon ton, for ninety dollars a month. While tending to Mr. Ford's children and ailing wife, Winnie Ruth became friendly with a neighboring family, the Hallorans. It would be a friendship destined to haunt the rest of her days.

The lure of a thirty-five-dollar-a-month raise—and perhaps the influence of Agnes Anne LeRoi, an x-ray technician who rented the other half of the duplex with her invalid girlfriend, Hedvig "Sammy" Samuelson—took Winnie Ruth to the new Grunow Clinic on East McDowell Road, where she began work as a doctor's receptionist the very day the clinic opened. LeRoi, called Anne, worked there as well.

Holding true to pattern, Dr. Judd did not fare as well. Unable to find employment in Phoenix, he set out for Los Angeles in the summer of 1931, where he sought a position in a clinic.

Meantime, Winnie Ruth and her neighbors had developed a fast friendship—later evidence would suggest a lesbian triangle—but shortly after the doctor's departure, Anne became ill and decided to return home to Oregon for a few months' stay. Winnie Ruth promptly moved in with Sammy.

But before taking up residence with Sammy, even before the doctor had left on his job search, Winnie Ruth had gotten entangled with Jack Halloran. According to her own admission, the torrid affair had begun on Christmas Eve 1930, and she fell passionately in love with him.

Married and with three children, Halloran was the owner of the Halloran-Bennett Lumber Company and was one of the most prosperous men in the Salt River Valley. A playboy par excellence, he was enormously popular among the social set. And perhaps for that reason his name, even today, is rarely found in print when the subject is Winnie Ruth and the odoriferous trunks. (As late as 1973, in a book written about the case, the authors—for reasons known only to them—rechristened Halloran, calling him "Carl Harris.")

In September, after an absence of six months, Anne returned to the Second Street duplex. Almost immediately, nerves quickened and tension heightened among the three women. After a time, Winnie Ruth decided it prudent to seek quarters elsewhere and rented an apartment at 1102 East Brill Street, just south of McDowell Road.

The move apparently eased whatever antagonism existed, and the trio continued their friendship, Halloran figuring prominently in the lives of each. According to testimony offered by Winnie Ruth during a psychiatric evaluation, "Happy Jack," as the press dubbed him at the time, visited the women almost every night, and his generosity enabled them to enjoy a lifestyle they otherwise could not have afforded. She told of countless parties at one residence or the other to which Halloran would bring extra men—friends and business associates—and plenty of illegal booze.

While proper folks did not speak about such things, it had long been a quiet Phoenix tradition that during the sweltering months of summer, well-heeled men would send their families off to cooler climes. Then, to ease their burden of loneliness, they would take "summer wives." Winnie Ruth and her girlfriends were conspicuous members of that sorority.

Trouble began when Halloran planned a hunting trip into Arizona's White Mountains. In a gesture quite uncharacteristic of a woman "passionately" in love, Winnie Ruth told him about an attractive young nurse at the Grunow Clinic who knew the mountains well. Intrigued, Halloran asked to meet her, and Winnie Ruth agreed to arrange it. She invited Lucille Moore to dine with them on the evening of October 15. They picked her up in Halloran's automobile, and en route to dinner, he insisted they stop by for a visit with Anne and Sammy.

Winnie Ruth, knowing how jealous her friends could be of other women, wanted Moore's presence to go undetected. She protested to Halloran and refused to leave the car. Moore remained with her while he went in alone. He soon returned and, much to Winnie Ruth's chagrin, was followed by two male friends, as well as Anne and Sammy, who generously urged everyone to stay for dinner. Winnie Ruth said they had other plans; the men got into the vehicle, and off they went to the Brill Street apartment—without Anne and Sammy.

The next evening, Anne invited Winnie Ruth over for a game of cards.

She was insistent, but Winnie Ruth declined, citing typing that had to be done for the office. But in truth, she was anticipating an evening alone with Halloran.

After waiting until almost nine o'clock, she realized she had been stood up and decided to catch the last trolley to Second Street. Anne and Sammy, as often they did, invited her to spend the night with them. She accepted, and the threesome undressed and got into their bedclothes. With a glass of milk in hand, Winnie Ruth curled up on the foot of Sammy's bed.

"Anne was sitting over on her bed, and we were talking...." So Winnie Ruth would tell authorities during a December 19, 1932, interview at the Arizona State Prison at Florence. "Anne said, 'Ruth, how did Jack Halloran ever meet Lucille Moore?' And I said, 'Why, I introduced them,' and she pitched onto me for introducing Jack Halloran to a girl who had syphilis.... And we started quarreling over that ... and I told her that she certainly had no right to tell things outside the clinic, and oh, she threw up to me a lot of things."

The argument intensified, and according to Winnie Ruth's testimony, Anne said, "I could simply kill you for introducing Jack to some girl who has syphilis....

"I made some very nasty remarks to them," admitted Winnie Ruth. "I told the girls that 'every doctor in that clinic [Grunow] thinks you and Sammy are in love with each other.' ... I said I was going to tell the doctors at the clinic that they were perverts."

By then, the quarreling had escalated to something decidedly more than an argument among friends. Winnie Ruth had bruised a raw and sensitive nerve.

She left the bed, went to the kitchen, and placed her milk glass on the counter.

> Sammy came through the breakfast room door ... and she had the gun pointed right at my heart, and I grabbed ... the hand with the gun.... The kitchen table was right there by the door, and on the table was the bread knife right about at the same time she shot me through the hand.... I stabbed her once in the shoulder and once in the head, and the blade of the knife bent clear around ... and then we

dropped to the floor and I grabbed her and pushed her…and I yelled, "Give me that gun"…and I grabbed the gun, and her hand was yet on the trigger when that shot went through her chest…and then we both grappled on the floor for the gun … and then Anne yelled, "Shoot, Sammy, shoot"…and she got the ironing board…and she said "I will brain you," and she hit me with the ironing board over the head.…She would knock me flat on the floor with the ironing board, and we rolled around in that way.

In the midst of the continuing struggle, the gun discharged again— twice, one bullet hitting Sammy in the head, the other hitting Anne in the head. The shots were fired at such close range, powder burns were left around the wounds.

Later, the state would build its case on the theory that each woman had been brutally murdered as she slept and that Winnie Ruth's hand wound was self-inflicted as a ploy to support a claim of self-defense.

After the shooting, Winnie Ruth dressed hurriedly and, having no idea what else to do, returned to the Brill Street apartment to retrieve a pocketbook that contained her husband's Los Angeles telephone number. As she left the apartment to call Dr. Judd, Halloran's automobile pulled into the drive. He was intoxicated; she was hysterical. In what, at best, must have been a disjointed conversation, she rattled off what had happened. Halloran thought it was some sort of prank between the girls and did not believe her. Finally, at Winnie Ruth's urging, he agreed to drive to the duplex and see for himself.

The doubting Halloran was served a quick jolt of reality. "When I opened the door the lights were on," Winnie Ruth Judd would claim. "I had left them on.…[Halloran] went in and picked up Sammy, and he carried her in and laid her on Anne's bed.

"[He] wanted me to straighten things around in the kitchen and I couldn't do anything with one hand…and I wanted to call the doctor…and he advised me not to do that, he would tend to all this himself. Then he pulled the trunk [in] from the garage.…He left it in the kitchen…[and] he put Anne's body in the trunk.…

"He scared me of the police.…Why, he scared the life out of me…what it would mean to me and my family, to him and his family.... He told me not to call my husband or call the police, I must not mention this to anyone, that he would take care of it himself... that everything would be all right... to say absolutely nothing."

After a fitful night, Winnie Ruth, following Halloran's instructions, went to work the next morning. Those who asked were told her bandaged hand had been burned by an iron. Sometime around noon, Halloran called to inquire about the bullet wound. Had she done anything about it? She replied that she wanted to have it taken care of in Los Angeles, and "he thought it was a good idea for me to go... and he wanted me to take... [the trunk] to Los Angeles."

Winnie Ruth protested, insisting that she could never do such a thing; but Halloran was persuasive. At last, she agreed.

That evening, they met at the duplex. Winnie Ruth noticed immediately that the house had been cleaned and the beds made—and that a mattress was missing from one. She did not think much about it at the time.

It was then she learned that Sammy's body had been dismembered and placed in yet a second trunk. Halloran explained that Sammy had been "operated" on.

The trunks proved too heavy—in excess of four hundred pounds—to be taken to the train depot by express delivery, so, by her own account, Winnie Ruth repacked them, putting parts of Sammy's corpse in a valise. Then, saying she was off to Los Angeles to deliver trunks of medical books to her husband, she asked her landlord and his son to transport her baggage to the depot. They obliged.

One can only wonder at the thoughts flitting through Winnie Ruth's mind as she rode the rails—body parts in a satchel nearby—some four hundred miles to her destination.

Removing the trunks from the train at Union Station, a baggage handler, sensitive to their odor, was overcome by nausea. Then he noticed liquid oozing from one of the trunks that looked suspiciously like blood. Unnerved, he called his boss, A. B. Anderson, who instructed that the trunks not be released.

In time, a stunning young woman and her male companion came by to claim them. Anderson demanded that the trunks be opened for inspection.

With composure that belied fear, the woman replied that she would have to telephone her husband to bring the keys. With that, she and the man walked off.

Anderson waited four hours for their return, then placed a call to the Los Angeles Police Department. Squad cars converged on the scene, and officers opened the trunks. What the men saw was indeed an unpleasant surprise.

Jack Lefler, reporting for the Associated Press, wrote, "Inside the larger [trunk], partly covered with a blanket among a litter of papers and letters, was the nearly nude body of a young woman [Anne].

"In the smaller trunk was the lower part of a woman's [Sammy's] body, the legs severed at the knees. The upper part was found in a suitcase [Winnie Ruth's carry-on valise] which had been checked at the station."

Each woman had been shot, one dismembered; both stank. A simple check of the baggage slips determined that the steamer trunks had been shipped from Phoenix the previous day, October 19, 1931, by one Winnie Ruth Judd.

The condition of Sammy's body would be a source of controversy for decades to come. Lloyd Andrews, the prosecutor at Winnie Ruth's trial, told reporters years later that the body had been hacked to pieces by an amateur. Any notion to the contrary was "hogwash."

However, the jury foreman, who saw photos of the mutilated corpse only after the trial's completion, said, "It was done by somebody who knew how to do it. A professional."

The LAPD threw a massive dragnet over Los Angeles, but Winnie Ruth, knowing her scheme had gone awry, had effectively vanished into the bowels of the city. Later, she would tell police that she had spent one night hiding behind draperies in a department store and four nights in a vacant cottage on the grounds of a sanitarium, where she had once been treated for tuberculosis.

Burton J. McKinnell, Winnie Ruth's brother and the man to whom the trunks were addressed, was taken into police custody. Badly shaken, he readily admitted that he was the male companion who had accompanied Winnie Ruth to claim the trunks, adding that his sister had asked him to help her dump them into the Pacific. Winnie Ruth, said the brother, had told him the women had been killed in self-defense.

McKinnell told investigators that he had driven his sister to downtown Los Angeles, given her five dollars—all the money he had—and dropped her off. That, he said, was the last he had seen of her.

Sometime during her flight, Winnie Ruth scribbled out a confession on telegraph blanks and addressed it to her husband. It was the disjointed rambling of a woman out of control:

> I fired [at Sammy] twice I think and since Anne was going to blackmail me . . . I fired at her. . . . Doctor dear, I'm sorry Sammy shot me, whether it was the pain or what, I got the gun and killed her.

Winnie Ruth thought better of the confession—the press would call it the "drain pipe letter"—and flushed it down a toilet. It was, however, retrieved from the sewer, pieced together, and used as evidence at her trial.

Four days after her disappearance—after headlines about the "trunk murderess" had flashed around the globe—police received a call from an attorney representing Winnie Ruth's husband. They were given the address of a mortuary and told to be there at ten o'clock that night.

Officers arrived at the appointed hour to find Winnie Ruth reposed on a sofa, a bullet wound in her left hand.

Heavily armed lawmen escorted Winnie Ruth back to Arizona in a caravan of automobiles that stretched across the desert. But the scene awaiting them at Phoenix must have been as startling to them as it was to their prisoner. Some twenty thousand people lined the streets fighting for a glimpse of the notorious "butcher." An obscure twenty-six-year-old receptionist had become an international item.

"A thousand persons fought their way into the courthouse basement corridor, and milled about the doors in vain efforts to get into the little justice courtroom, which accommodates only seventy-five spectators," wrote the Associated Press on November 9, 1931, following a hearing that would be the first formality leading to a trial. The account noted that she was "attired in a long, clinging black dress, the pale of her face accentuated by lack of rouge or lipstick." It would be the first of hundreds of such accounts, and the circuslike atmosphere would prevail throughout the duration of the case.

Winnie Ruth was charged with murder in the first degree, and the trial was set to begin December 15. The defense protested, insisting the date would not allow sufficient time for preparation. Unmoved by such a trifle, the judge remained firm. However, a later motion was granted, and the trial got under way January 19, 1932.

It was a trial that gave a mesmerized public an offering of sex, lesbianism, murder, mutilation, money, and high society. Some argue that what it did not offer was a fair hearing of the accused.

Throughout the trial, Winnie Ruth begged with her attorneys to be allowed to take the stand in her own defense. They resolutely refused. She did not testify, and against her wishes, a plea of not guilty by reason of insanity was put before the court.

Jack Halloran was sworn in as a witness for the defense, and Winnie Ruth was convinced his testimony would exonerate her. He was never called to testify.

Initial news reports of the alleged murders stated that the police were convinced that more than one person was involved, and in fact, Maricopa County issued arrest warrants for Winnie Ruth and two John Does. This fact was not brought out in the proceedings.

Fingerprints were not made of bloodstains found in the house—which could have implicated another person or persons in the dismemberment of Sammy's body—and before the police concluded their investigation of the premises, the landlord was allowed to sell ten-cent tickets to a horde of people anxious to tour the home.

A bloodstained mattress was found in the desert two miles from the crime scene. Despite the fact that a mattress was missing from the duplex and the defendant did not know how to drive an automobile, no one asked to whom the mattress belonged to or how it got there.

In perhaps the most curious twist, Winnie Ruth was tried only for the death of Anne—whose body had not been mutilated. While the sensational aspect of the dismemberment of Sammy's body was put constantly before the jury, it was completely unnecessary to prove who had carved it up. And if Winnie Ruth had not done it, whoever had was never brought to trial, because Sammy's death was never brought to trial.

Winnie Ruth's husband, a known drug addict, testified that his wife was perhaps insane—that she was disposed to strange mood swings. He then sold stories about her to newspapers and magazines for as much as five thousand dollars each.

Another doctor testified that indeed Winnie Ruth was insane. But the prosecution psychiatrist testified that she was not–thus inching open the gate to the gallows.

The flamboyant Hearst newspapers got into the act, claiming the state had suppressed letters and diaries of the victims, the contents of which would, if revealed, blow the lid off Phoenix society. No such items surfaced in the courtroom.

Throughout much of the trial, the defendant remained stoic, looking ahead and twisting a handkerchief in her hands, but now and again, the proceedings would be interrupted by boisterous outbursts. On one occasion, Winnie Ruth broke free of the matron, shoved the court psychiatrist against the wall, and kicked the county sheriff. The incident did little to endear her to the jury.

On February 8, 1932, following twenty-one grueling days of testimony, just two hours and forty minutes were taken by the all-male jury to reach a verdict of murder in the first degree. Medical testimony about the angle of the bullets as they entered the women's bodies had convinced the jurors that Anne and Sammy were shot as they slept.

"Mrs. Ruth Judd Convicted; Jury Fixes Death Penalty," read the headline of the February 9, 1932, *Arizona Republic*. Beneath the bold splash of letters is a striking photograph of a determined young woman. Her large oval eyes are alert and penetrating, her mouth drawn into a tight line. To the right of this remarkable photo is a subhead: "Defendant Calm as Decision of Peers is Read to Crowded Court Room."

On February 24, 1932, Winnie Ruth was sentenced to hang by the neck until dead. She did not remain stoic but erupted like a waking volcano. "Those women were not murdered," she shrieked. "You're trying to hang me, and I won't have it. I didn't cut those bodies. I couldn't do it."

That said, prisoner number 8811 was shuffled off to a condemned cell at the penitentiary in Florence.

Ten months after Winnie Ruth's death sentence was imposed, Jack Halloran was charged as an accessory to murder and released on three thousand dollars bond. A preliminary hearing was set early in January.

With the confidence of a grandee who knew his place well in Phoenix society, Halloran told reporters, "The grievousness of my deeds consists of no greater fault than having been indiscreet." The charges were tossed out of court on a legal technicality.

Renz Jennings Sr. thought the ruling was a miscarriage of justice, and when he became Maricopa County attorney, he filed charges against Halloran of "aiding and assisting" Winnie Ruth in disposing of the bodies, of "aiding, assisting, and advising her to conceal the slayings and of encouraging her to escape from Arizona to California."

With brazen duplicity, Halloran's attorneys argued that Winnie Ruth had proved she had killed Anne and Sammy in self-defense, which, of course, was not a crime; therefore, Halloran was not an accessory to anything.

Most astonishing was the judge's decision. In what must be the most convoluted ruling ever handed down by an Arizona magistrate, Judge J. C. Niles said, "The state of Arizona has definitely proved that Mrs. Judd acted in self-defense. Therefore, there was no crime committed."

The ruling begs an elementary question. If the state was convinced Winnie Ruth had acted in self-defense—which is not a crime—why, then, had she been convicted of first-degree murder and imprisoned to await the hangman's noose? The Niles ruling leaves open a myriad of questions yet to be answered.

"I had previously had some experience with the judge who tried . . . [Winnie Ruth's] case," wrote Jennings in his memoirs, "and I felt that his 'stinger' was out for me. In addition, before the trial was over, I felt that he had some kind of close relationship with . . . [Halloran]. Thus the accused was not bound over for trial."

Jennings had called Winnie Ruth as his star witness, and it is possible that Niles was influenced by her courtroom behavior. Authors J. Dwight Dobkins and Robert J. Hendricks, who proved themselves apologists for Halloran by renaming him Carl Harris, wrote that Winnie Ruth "time after time electrified the courtroom gallery of two hundred spectators with startling revelations, hysterical outbursts and verbal attacks on Carl Harris. And time and again many of her statements were ordered stricken from the official court record . . . [by Judge Niles]."

If anything positive came from the judge's bizarre ruling, it was the glimmer of hope given Winnie Ruth and her attorneys that the death sentence imposed on her might be commuted.

When the Arizona Board of Pardons and Paroles met in March 1933, it had before it more than thirty-five hundred recommendations of leniency, including petitions signed by thirty state legislators and statements from four of Winnie Ruth's jurors. Things appeared hopeful.

"If the evidence and facts now brought to light had been produced from the witness stand during the trial," wrote jury foreman Stewart Thompson in his affidavit, "there would have been sufficient doubt raised in my mind as to whether or not Agnes [Anne] LeRoi had been killed in self-defense that I would have recommended a penalty of life imprisonment."

This and other affidavits were compelling documents, but they were written in vain. The board upheld the death sentence and set the execution date for April 28.

According to the Associated Press, Winnie Ruth "was stunned" when her seventy-three-year-old father broke the news to her in her cell, but she "accepted the news calmly." If one is to take the story at face value, then it seems the condemned woman was stunned into a state of calm.

"If it is God's will," intoned the retired preacher with more than a little piety, "it is for the best."

Many argued, however, that the good reverend had confused God with the parole board.

The next day, the AP broke the story of a botched escape attempt. "Prison authorities confirmed a statement made in Los Angeles by Burt McKinnell, Mrs. Judd's brother, that a saw had been delivered to the condemned woman. She used it, they revealed, to saw through one of five bars criss-crossing the window of her little adobe, one-room house in the yard of the women's ward."

The activity was halted when authorities discovered the eight-inch hacksaw blade "with which she had attacked the steel."

Held briefly by Los Angeles police, McKinnell was released after the state of Arizona declared it had no interest in him.

The single hope left to Winnie Ruth was a sanity hearing, and in a move that surprised many, Warden A. C. Walker petitioned the state to conduct one. It did, and seventy-two hours before her scheduled walk to the gallows, a Pinal County jury judged her insane. With swiftness rivaling the jury decision that had found her guilty of murder, Winnie Ruth was transferred to the State Hospital at Twenty-Fourth Street and Van Buren in Phoenix.

The immediate threat was lifted, but Winnie Ruth continued to walk in the shadow of death: if at any time she was judged to have regained sanity, a new execution date would be set.

A model patient who assisted nurses at the understaffed institution and dabbled as a hairdresser, Winnie Ruth was little heard of for the next half-dozen years until 1939, when she wandered away from the hospital. After six days, she was captured and, according to the *Phoenix Gazette*, was "half-starved and hysterical."

But she was not hysterical enough to stay put. Six weeks later, headlines splashed the news that Winnie Ruth was gone again. This adventure lasted twelve days and was accorded press coverage reminiscent of that given machine-gun-toting gangsters.

After an eight-year hiatus, she escaped for twelve hours in 1947 and thirteen hours in 1951. Each time she wandered away, much ado was made in the newspapers. When she made her fifth attempt in 1952, it was reported that she had "slid down an improvised rope from a third story tower of the ward. She apparently scaled a nine-foot fence topped by three strands of wire.

"Four employees say a black 1948 Hudson was parked as close as possible to Judd's ward," the story concluded, implying that the Hudson was a getaway car.

Years later, Winnie Ruth, in a unique interview, would tell a Phoenix journalist that each escape—including a sixth in 1952—was facilitated by a key, always in her possession, to the front door of the institution. She simply unlocked the door and left.

Winnie Ruth's first significant victory occurred as a result of her February 3, 1952, disappearance. While on the lam, she asked a friend to call hospital director M. W. Conway and tell him that she would surrender if permitted to appear before a grand jury. The administrator agreed, a grand jury was called, and she returned as promised.

Following one of her many escapes, Winnie Ruth talks to Yuma County Sheriff T.H. Newman.

On February 11, 1952, she offered four hours of closed-door testimony. Her argument of self-defense and her statement of Halloran's involvement in the dismemberment and attempted disposal of the bodies were so persuasive the grand jury recommended that her death sentence be commuted to life imprisonment. The parole board agreed with the recommendation, and Governor Howard Pyle signed the order on May 11, 1952.

After more than two decades, Winnie Ruth at last had told her story to a jury. And after more than two decades, the fear of execution had been lifted. But something in the scheme of Arizona justice was still askew. Winnie Ruth had convinced a jury that she had acted in self-defense; she had been in confinement longer than most of the nation's convicted murderers; yet still there was no end in sight.

Psychiatrists had long since determined she was harmless, and several recommendations were made that her sentence be commuted to time served, but another decade rolled by, and nothing—short of promises from a variety of state officials—happened. Finally, Winnie Ruth's patience ebbed, and she took matters in hand. On October 8, 1962—for the first time in a decade—she inserted her key in the hospital's front door and walked away.

Assisted by friends and family, she made her way to Northern California, took the name Marian Lane, and, for the next six-and-a-half years, lived in a mansion in Piedmont, where she served as a maid and became the devoted companion of a wealthy doctor and his wife.

The magnanimous couple promised to provide for Winnie Ruth for the rest of her life, and when she reached sixty-five years of age, a cottage was refurbished for her at the family farm. It was there, on June 27, 1969, that the dream of a kinder life unraveled. Winnie Ruth, a.k.a. Marion Lane, was taken into police custody. No one could have been more surprised than her benefactors, who did not have a clue about her real identity. And no one could have been more supportive.

One of the nation's best-known defense lawyers, Melvin Belli, was hired to handle her case, and he in turn hired Phoenix attorney Larry Debus to serve as Arizona counsel.

Belli argued extradition eyeball-to-eyeball with California governor Ronald Reagan, but the former thespian was unmoved by Winnie Ruth's plight, and she was returned to Arizona.

According to journalist Jana Bommersback, who investigated the case in depth, Debus' "first tactic was to do something few defense lawyers ever do: get his client into prison."

The attorney's logic was simple. The only way to get Winnie Ruth a pardon was to get her out of the hospital and into prison.

Pointing out that she had served twenty-nine-and-a-half years and that most people serving life sentences were back on the streets in eight to ten years, Attorney General Gary Nelson argued that Winnie Ruth must be given credit for the years she had spent in the state hospital.

With Debus and Belli in her corner, Winnie Ruth appeared before the parole board on October 27, 1969. Four days later, hope was dashed when the board voted two to one to deny parole.

Citing excessive privileges granted Winnie Ruth at the state hospital, the ruling read, in part, "To observe the application of punishment in this case from beginning to end, one wonders if it could not be singled out as the case more disposed to induce and encourage crime, rather than act as a preventive."

Belli was outraged. "They should have been born at the time of the Inquisition," he said of the board.

Almost a year and a half had passed when, on February 16, 1971, the parole board met again to determine Winnie Ruth's fate. Dr. Otto Bendheim, who had known and treated her for more than thirty years, testified that she was "sound, sane, and absolutely harmless. She presents no danger whatever to society or to herself. There are no suicidal, homicidal, or violent tendencies. She has a potential for constructive and meaningful contributions to society."

Again the vote was two to one but this time the board recommended to Governor Jack Williams that her sentence be commuted. Just before Christmas 1971, Williams signed the necessary documents, and Winnie Ruth was spirited away to California in the dead of night, a legally free woman for the first time in forty years but with a curious stipulation attached to her release: that she never tell her story "or any part thereof."

"She is guilty of the most cold-blooded murder I ever encountered," commented prosecutor Lloyd Andrews many years after her trial. "If ever anyone deserved to be hanged, it is she."

"If the bodies had not been mutilated [Anne's had not, but the perception fostered by the prosecution prevailed] after the crime," wrote O. G. Murrow, publisher of the *Ash Fork Record*, in a 1933 letter to the parole board, "I do not believe a verdict of first degree would have been brought in. And it seems to me that the death sentence was imposed, not because of the crime itself, but because of the means used to dispose of the bodies."

Some experts who have examined evidence and trial testimony agree that if the case had been tried today, Winnie Ruth probably would have been convicted of manslaughter and sentenced to a year or two in jail at most.

Winnie Ruth lived for a while in the cottage at the doctor's farm, then moved to her own apartment in Stockton, California, where she took up gardening and joined a church.

Nearly two decades after her release from custody, she spoke with *Arizona Republic* reporter Randy Collier in a voice described as "frail" and "sickly": "You know, I'm eighty-five-years-old now. I just had a birthday. I'm not pretty anymore. I'm all stoop-shouldered. I don't think anyone would think I'm pretty now. I don't really want stories [written] about me. I want people to like me."

Some people may; others may not. But as long as stories are written, the name of Winnie Ruth Judd will find a reader interested in her tale.

Chapter 13

The Raid on Short Creek

IT IS A HARSH LAND of broad plateaus, ominous canyons and jagged cliffs, punctuated here and there by bleak volcanic hills. Isolated in the northwestern corner of Arizona, abutting Utah and Nevada and roughly the size of Delaware, Connecticut, and Rhode Island combined, it is one of the state's most inaccessible and least-populated regions. It is called the Arizona Strip.

There, on the Kaibab Plateau, some twenty-five miles from Pipe Spring and forty miles from Fredonia and the nearest telephone, sat the tiny village of Short Creek. And there, in the predawn blackness of July 26, 1953, occurred the largest police action undertaken in Arizona in modern times.

Established in 1909, Short Creek was an obscure hamlet without distinguishing characteristics until 1928, when brothers Price and Elmer Johnson moved their families from Lee's Ferry on the Colorado River to the remote community in the hope of continuing, without societal interference, their practice of polygamy. In time, Short Creek would become a mecca for renegade polygamy, which had been outlawed nearly a century before by the federal government. The Church of Jesus Christ of Latterday Saints had disavowed the practice by manifesto in 1890. Outside of the law and without the sanction of the Mormon church, plural unions nevertheless continued to manifest themselves among men and women steeped in the fundamentalist belief in its sanctity. Cut off from the mainstream of civilization, the geography of the Arizona Strip offered the fundamentalists an appealing sanctuary.

Short Creek's inhabitants asked little of the world. The men worked small farms while the women tended their large families. Cows and chickens were raised in a communal effort, and each family was provided for according to its needs. Homes were simple dwellings of weathered pine boards, lacking electricity and indoor plumbing. The town's most substantial structure, and the single building with electricity, served a dual purpose as school and church. On weekdays, the children learned to read and write. On Sundays, they learned the fundamentalist principals that guided their elders. Boys were taught that salvation was achieved by taking multiple wives, while girls were taught that their purpose in life was to serve their husbands—and to multiply and replenish the earth.

Isolated as Short Creek was, its residents lived with the nagging dread of unwanted interference. And they had precedent for their apprehension. The state had raided the village in 1935, and in 1944 a second raid was conducted with the FBI. In both instances, men were convicted of various charges (mostly Mann Act violations), but the majority of convictions were overturned on legal technicalities, and only a handful of men ever saw the inside of a jail. The raids were unsettling and disruptive but did nothing to dampen the religious fervor that held the sect together as a cohesive group. If anything, the raids made martyrs of those arrested.

The polygamists at Short Creek were a close-mouthed lot; nonetheless, it was widely known along the Arizona Strip that wives in the community shared their husbands with other women. But most outsiders simply shrugged off the knowledge and went about their business, allowing the polygamists to live as they saw fit. It might have remained that way had it not been for the keen eyes of welfare workers in Kingman, the Mohave County seat some four hundred miles distant. It seems that women in Short

Short Creek as it looked in 1953.

Creek were applying for assistance for their children and, in many cases, listing the same man as husband and father. At first, it was dismissed as a curious coincidence, but in time, it became apparent that something odd was occurring at Short Creek.

When it was learned that some of the wives applying for welfare were as young as thirteen and fourteen, the authorities became alarmed. Arizona law stipulated that no girl under the age of sixteen could marry, and if a girl younger than that became pregnant, it was grounds for a charge of statutory rape.

The troublesome situation at Short Creek came to the attention of high-level officials when, in March 1951, Superior Court Judge J. W. Faulkner approached Governor Howard Pyle and Attorney General Fred Wilson to suggest a grand jury investigation be conducted. Wilson weighed the matter and decided more direct action should be taken. He proposed that the state of Arizona, in conjunction with Utah, raid Short Creek. The notion was not nixed, but each man agreed that nothing could be done prior to obtaining unshakable proof.

The Arizona legislature appropriated ten thousand dollars for investigative purposes, and the state hired the Burns Detective Agency to ferret out information. It would be an ongoing process for the next twenty-four months.

By 1953 Short Creek had blossomed into a community of 368 inhabitants. Seventy-one adults and 209 children lived on the Arizona side of the border, while 34 adults and 54 children lived on the Utah side. Of the combined populations, 15 were girls fourteen to eighteen years of age who were married with children. It was the existence of these dubious marriages that authorities found most disconcerting.

By the spring of 1952, the Burns detectives had mapped the entire town and labeled each home with the names of its occupants. Wilson determined it was time to act and scheduled a raid for the middle of June. It was his intention to uproot the entire community, move the inhabitants to Kingman, and incarcerate them in barracks to await court proceeding—thus eliminating the problem at Short Creek by eliminating Short Creek itself.

But the governor's more level head prevailed, and Wilson's bizarre plan was scrapped. The June raid was scuttled.

As the months came and went, the thorn of Short Creek dug deeper into the sides of Mohave County authorities, who pressed the capitol for action. Pyle called a meeting between himself, Ross Jones (Wilson's successor as attorney general), and Mohave County Sheriff Frank Porter. Each agreed that a raid must be staged, but each also agreed that it must be staged in the most humane manner possible. It was, after all, no small thing to remove babies from the arms of their mothers and to separate families. And the cry of religious persecution was not a sound the state was anxious to hear.

Pyle later would assert that the raid on Short Creek was "the one and only real sorrow of my administration."

The governor and the attorney general held secret sessions with the house and senate appropriations committees, and fifty thousand dollars was allotted for the raid under the guise of "grasshopper" control. One misguided legislator, unable to distinguish between the fundamentalists and mainstream Mormons, suggested the raid be dubbed "Operation Seagull"– a crude reference to the Latter-day Saints' first summer in the Salt Lake Valley, when seagulls devoured thousands of grasshoppers, thus saving the new settlers' crops and averting certain starvation.

Pyle then called Governor J. Bracken Lee of Utah, one of the West's most controversial politicians, to seek cooperation and advice. Lee wisely declined to participate in the actual raid, but, through his attorney general, made arrangements to cooperate in any extradition proceedings that might result. His cooperation, however, was contingent upon Pyle's agreement to allow Utah authorities to monitor the raid. Pyle readily agreed.

Next, Pyle revealed his plans to David O. McKay, president of the Mormon Church in Salt Lake City. The governor knew that the church bore no responsibility for the polygamous practices of a breakaway sect and wanted McKay to understand that Arizona had the utmost respect for its Latter-day Saint residents and neighbors.

Thousands of hours were spent in preparation for the raid. All parties involved agreed that it must be nonviolent and to insure that harm would come to no one, an overwhelming force must be used. Sheriff Porter insisted that two officers be assigned to each house in the village, thus a force of at least one hundred men would be employed.

Polygamist wife and children.

That was the easy part. In order to assure the general public that Arizona officials were indeed humane, it would be necessary to exercise measures to safeguard Short Creek's population during the raid and during the occupation of the town. Arresting the adults meant that the younger wives and children would have to be cared for. In addition, provisions had to be made to feed and shelter a team of welfare workers, matrons, doctors, nurses, and more than one hundred law-enforcement officers. Ultimately, it would be necessary to provide for the needs of some six hundred people and to do so under makeshift conditions in blistering July heat.

Plans included the erection of a large mess tent and other tents to accommodate medical personnel, as well as the provision of a radio communications center and a mobile power station. Men and vehicles were borrowed from the Arizona National Guard. The military insignia on trucks were carefully painted over and the soldiers were paid out of a special fund. The raid, after all, was a civil action, and no politician wanted the impression created that the state was conducting a military action against a defenseless town.

Prosecutors prepared 122 arrest warrants, and on July 1, Pyle declared that a state of insurrection existed at Short Creek, a formality that gave legality to the state's plan of action.

Despite that not-so-subtle warning to Short Creek's polygamists, the state decided that at midnight the night of the raid, the phone line at Fredonia—forty miles away but the nearest town—would be cut to minimize forewarning.

On Saturday, July 25, 1953, startled residents of Williams, a small town 125 miles south of Short Creek, watched an armada of highway patrol cars descend on the street fronting the high school auditorium. Townsfolk counted sixty in all. In addition, thirty deputies had arrived from Mohave County, and twelve liquor-control officers (never mind that the fundamentalists forbade the use of alcohol) rounded out the group. Each man in the armada thought he was there to attend traffic patrol school. The residents of Williams had been told nothing. They did not have the slightest notion why such an army of law-enforcement officers had invaded their community.

After the lawmen were assembled in the auditorium, the ruse was revealed. Air National Guard maps of Short Creek were shown the men, then they were divided into squads and given maps of the village, with each house numbered in red.

At nightfall, the patrol cars departed Williams at five-minute intervals. Hoping to cut Short Creek off from both directions, one group of vehicles proceeded east to Flagstaff, then north to Navajo Bridge at Marble Canyon. The other group drove northwest toward Nevada in order to reach the village through Hurricane on the Utah side. Speed was set at fifty miles per hour, and the estimated time of arrival was set at four o'clock Sunday morning.

But despite countless hours of planning and preparation, it mattered little what time the officers arrived. The veil of secrecy shrouding the mission was all for naught. Sometime around one o'clock in the morning, a loose-tongued newsman drove into Short Creek and asked the first person he found, "Has the raid happened yet?"

There was no panic and little surprise, just resignation and an end to the nagging dread each member of the community had lived with. Observers were posted on the vermilion cliffs above town, a dynamite blast awakened the community to its fate, and leaders of the sect assembled on the school-yard lawn to await their intruders.

All at once, the blazing headlights of patrol cars, National Guard trucks, and news vehicles could be seen approaching the town from either direction. Moments later, they rolled onto Short Creek's unpaved main street, sirens whaling, red lights flashing, and dust rising in furious swirls against the coal-black sky.

Sheriff Porter left his vehicle, and armed with arrest warrants and accompanied by Attorney General Jones, he approached the sect's leader, who told him that the polygamists had run for the last time. He explained that if it was necessary, his people would "stand right here and shed our blood."

No one will ever know if the threat was serious or merely bluster, but his words created a tense moment. "You're friends of mine," said Porter. "You've known me for years. We don't want violence, but we're here to do a job, and we're going to get it done."

No blood was shed. There was no violence. In half an hour, Short Creek was declared "secure."

"The multiple families of polygamous Short Creek were split asunder today by the wrath of Arizona," reported the *Prescott Evening Courier* with words chosen carefully to nip at the heels of authorities.

"We have done no wrong," asserted another of Short Creek's leaders, as a reporter for the Associated Press scribbled down his words. "We just practice our religion according to our beliefs."

Arizona had launched a massive, complicated, costly police action in order to accomplish what Sheriff Porter and a few deputies probably could have done on their own.

"Outside of Russia and Red China," wrote the *Courier* in a blistering editorial that also noted the truce signed in Korea the day following the raid on Short Creek, "the whole world gasped in wonder at the feat of arms.

"The 'revolutionaries' seemed ready for hostilities," it continued with marked sarcasm. "A cache of dynamite was uncovered, guns were found in homes, while youngsters were flinging volleyballs and other bouncing missiles about. There likely were pitchforks, axes, hatchets, hoes and shovels, pick handles and butcher knives available, though the furtiveness of the foray prevented their use when the time for action came. Yet, it was a glorious triumph, a faster and better one than the nation and its puny allies scored in Korea."

The *Courier* was not alone in its scorn. The *Arizona Republic*, seething with indignation, wrote, "We say officials of the State of Arizona have humiliated its citizens by a pistol and shotgun raid that resembled an operation to subdue Pork Chop Hill."

As residents reluctantly answered—or avoided answering—questions put to them by law-enforcement officers, the National Guardsmen were busy patching together a radio link to Phoenix.

"Rathole Number One to Rathole Number Two," called a soldier in a microphone.

Rathole Number Two was the unlikely designation given the headquarters in the capital where Governor Pyle anxiously awaited news about the outcome of the raid and where the former radio announcer would take to the air to explain to his constituents the reasoning behind such a dramatic police action.

At nine that morning, reported the *Arizona Republic*, Pyle leaned into a microphone in Phoenix and said, "Arizona has mobilized and used its total police power to protect the lives and future of 263 children. They are the products and the victims of the foulest conspiracy you could possibly imagine. More than one hundred peace officers...have arrested almost the entire population of a community dedicated to the production of white slaves who are without hope of escaping this degrading slavery from the moment of their birth...highly competent investigators have been unable to find a single instance in the last decade of a girl reaching the age of fifteen without having been forced into a shameful mockery of marriage."

It was a compelling speech that produced shockwaves among Arizonans unaware of the polygamist colony at Short Creek. But to many residents of northern Arizona—people long aware of the fundamentalists' unshakable belief in the religious sanctity of polygamy—it rang as spurious verbiage designed to justify a costly action from which no lasting good results could be had. As a Flagstaff man would later say, "It was a damned waste of time and money."

Pyle's concern for the children of Short Creek was shared by a correspondent for the Associated Press, but the reporter's prose indicates bafflement about a state that waited so long to take action, then acted with such élan. "[The children] seemed to ask what was it all about, this thing they were enmeshed in. This thing their parents had gotten them into. This strange, invisible force that was tearing their community apart with silent, anguished convulsions.

"Somehow they were pawns in this game that the state of Arizona said must now be played according to the rules."

Superior Court Judge J. Smith Gibbons read men and women their rights, then sent them off to the county jail at Kingman. Young women with small children were released on their own recognizance and allowed to return to their dwellings. Two other superior court judges, Lorna Lockwood and Faulkner, sat as a juvenile court and took jurisdiction over every child on the Arizona side of the town, including twelve juvenile wives.

The next week proved to be a nightmare of predictability. Fifteen officers were left to police the community, but they were no match for a group of women deprived of jailed husbands. One night, ten women and children crossed over the Utah border. The following night, another ten disappeared. Then ten women and forty children turned up missing. Short of their voluntary return, the onus was on Utah to extradite each of the women and to care for the juvenile children.

On August 1, forty-three thousand dollars in bail was posted at Kingman, and the jailed men were released and returned to Short Creek. But it was not the homecoming they had looked forward to. Unbeknownst to them, five Greyhound buses had come to town earlier that day and whisked away their families to uncertain destinations in Phoenix.

The five buses, accompanied by twelve patrol cars, deposited 154 children and thirty-eight mothers four hundred miles from their homes on the steps of the Department of Public Welfare, where they were shuffled off to various locations scattered throughout the valley.

Sitting in Phoenix, Superior Court Judge Lockwood announced that no child would be separated from its mother. Foster homes were found among sympathetic families, where the young mothers and their children were cared for.

While the husbands at Short Creek remained free on bail, a myriad of legal problems plagued authorities. Proceedings were postponed time and again because of technicalities, and the preliminary hearing—like the eventual trials—would have to be held in Phoenix. Bringing the defendants to trial in Mohave County was out of the question. Had the defense demanded a separate trial for each of the 107 defendants, some eight thousand jurors would have to be called. That would have been no small feat in a county of roughly nine thousand citizens.

Nearly a year had passed since the raid when thirty-six men pleaded guilty to a conspiracy to violate the state's laws—such as they were—against polygamy. Each man was given a one-year suspended sentence, the bench cognizant that to lock them away would effectuate martyrdom. But despite its legal restraint, the state had unwittingly bestowed martyrdom already—with a seeming vengeance.

The juvenile mothers and children in foster homes in Phoenix were forbidden ever to return to Short Creek. But many—if not most—did return after they reached maturity and were outside of the jurisdiction of juvenile court.

What purpose was served by this massive raid on Short Creek? Virtually none at all—other than to give folks in towns along the Arizona Strip, and across the border in Utah, tales to tell future generations.

The passage of four decades has changed little along the Arizona Strip. It is a harsh land of broad plateaus, ominous canyons, and jagged cliffs—one of the most inaccessible and least-populated regions of the state. Callused hands and sturdy backs scratch up survival from sun-baked earth unblessed by rain—and the cycle of life and death goes on unchanged, for that is the nature of things with people who ask little and expect less.

Today, Short Creek is called Colorado City; the Utah side, Hilldale. Together, they have a population of about thirty-five hundred. Dust trailing from behind unfamiliar vehicles is looked upon with interest. Strangers are regarded with skepticism—and questions about polygamy go unanswered.

Chapter 14

An Alias for Any Occasion

HE DIDN'T SEEM THE TYPE. Described as "sharp of feature," Dr. William E. Estaver—or so he called himself—was slight of build, spectacled, and partial to Norfolk jackets, stiff collars, puttees, and straw hats. He was a literate man, well-spoken, friendly, and persuasive, and claimed to be a dentist from Detroit. Some called him a dandy. The state of Arizona called him a killer.

It was November 14, 1921, when Estaver registered at the Willard Hotel in Tucson under the name J. C. Beck, ostensibly to avoid an acquaintance down on his luck who wanted to borrow money from him. During his brief stay, he would be remembered for telling fanciful stories and making a nuisance of himself.

While J. N. McCain, a barber on East Congress Street, trimmed his hair, Estaver volunteered that he had just walked across the desert from Ajo, Arizona, where his automobile had broken down. When the skeptical barber asked how he had managed such quick time, his customer replied that he had taken a twenty-mile shortcut across the mountains. It was not the first time a tall tale had emanated from the lips of a man seated in McCain's porcelain barber's chair. He shrugged it off and went about the business of clipping.

It is not clear why the natty little man shared such a tale with the barber, but it is clear that the story was a fabrication. Estaver had come to Tucson from Phoenix—where he had stopped at the St. Francis Hotel under the name "August Pick"—and had ventured south in the comfort of a railroad coach.

The odd thing about the story was that some three weeks before Estaver's red Sheridan roadster had broken down near Ajo, at Sentinel.

Rather than wait for repairs to be made, he had gone by train to Los Angeles, leaving the vehicle to be fixed by mechanic O. B. Anderson. Anderson then was hired to drive the car to Los Angeles, where he and Estaver enjoyed a two-day sightseeing excursion. Estaver sold the roadster, telling the mechanic he intended to purchase a touring car. It was all quite strange.

William Knelange, custodian of the Tucson Auto Park on Fremont Avenue, was another to have an odd exchange with Estaver. Guests complained, wrote the *Star*, "because . . . [he] was going from tourist to tourist trying to get a ride to the coast." When confronted by the custodian, the vaunting dentist repeated the story of a vehicle broken down in the desert but embellished the anecdote by declaring that his wife was waiting for him to return with parts to repair the automobile. To add credence to his story, Estaver produced a photograph of himself and a woman posing beside a disabled roadster. Unmoved by the stranger's narrative, Knelange ordered Estaver out of the park.

Peter Johnson, described by the *Star* as an "exceedingly large man weighing well over two hundred pounds," and his portly wife, Anna, would be next to encounter the dapper raconteur. A contractor from Denver who spoke with a thick Swedish accent, the sixty-year-old Johnson and his wife of forty were on an extended holiday, motoring leisurely to Los Angeles in their newly purchased Dodge touring car, when they stopped in Tucson for the night. A man of prudent temperament, Johnson wanted the best protection available for his automobile and sought out the McArthur Brothers Dodge agency at the southwest corner of Broadway and Scott Avenue. While he was inside arranging overnight storage for the vehicle, Anna found herself in conversation with an engaging stranger who introduced himself as "Buckmaster."

When Johnson returned to the car, he was told that the talkative tramontane had a broken-down "machine" at Sentinel and a wife waiting for him there. He had come to Tucson to purchase "repairing materials" and had promised his worried spouse a speedy return. He had approached a taxi service, but the driver wanted to charge him eighty dollars for the trip, a sum he considered exorbitant. Would it be possible for him to ride along with the Johnsons?

Impossible, he was told. Johnson intended to take the Phoenix-Blythe-

Mecca road, and Sentinel was on another route altogether. Not to be dissuaded, the stranger drew a photograph from the pocket of his Norfolk jacket and handed it to the unyielding man. It showed an automobile stuck in the sand on what the stranger said was on the Phoenix-Blythe-Mecca route, a dreadful road that was certain to do damage to Johnson's prized Dodge. The Ajo-Sentinel-Yuma route was over a vastly superior roadway.

Johnson was having none of it and said that he "could not carry anyone, since the machine was overloaded as it was." The stranger was disappointed by the refusal but gracious enough to recommend the Willard Hotel when the couple inquired about lodging for the night.

For reasons that remain obscure, Johnson—perhaps at his wife's urging—later changed his mind and decided to offer the man a ride. After all, the fellow was a friendly sort, well-groomed, and seemingly harmless enough. Johnson approached Carey Cox, proprietor of the Willard, and asked for the room number of a Mr. Buckmaster. Cox searched the hotel register, but no one by that name had checked in. Perplexed, Johnson described the man he sought, and Cox linked the description to a J. C. Beck, the alias under which Estaver had registered earlier that day.

"At about nine or ten o'clock that night," wrote the *Star*, "he came knocking at my door," Johnson later recounted. It was agreed that Pick-Beck-Buckmaster-Estaver would be given a ride to Sentinel if he would pay to have a trunk shipped by rail to Los Angeles. Eliminating the trunk would create passenger space on the backseat of the Johnson automobile.

Estaver readily agreed, and the two men carried the trunk down the street and around the corner to the Southern Pacific depot, where Estaver paid $5.40 expressage, a paltry sum when compared to the value of Johnson's new Dodge touring car and the wad of cash that must be in the old man's wallet; Estaver intended to relieve him of both.

Unbeknownst to either man, the events to follow would precipitate one of the lengthiest and most bizarre criminal cases tried in the history of Pima County Superior Court and dramatically alter the future for both Johnson and Estaver.

Early the next morning, the improbable trio loaded itself into Johnson's Dodge and set out across a vast stretch of desert notable for its emptiness and isolation. It became evident at once that the Ajo-Sentinel-Yuma route followed a roadway that was, at its best, primitive and, at its worst, little more than a rutted dirt trail wholly unsuitable for the fragile balloon tires carrying the massive vehicle's weight. Given Johnson's original plan to take the Phoenix-Blythe-Mecca route, it is fair to assume that considerable grumbling accompanied the dust kicked up from the desert floor.

Averaging some ten miles per hour, the party traveled all day, arriving at Ajo late in the afternoon. The New Cornelia Hotel was an inviting sight, and the Johnsons proposed that they stay overnight and continue on in the morning. Estaver protested. Sentinel was only about forty miles west. His wife was staying with friends there. He knew she was worried about him, and he was anxious to complete the trip. It would be of at least small benefit to the Johnsons: his wife's friends would accommodate the party at no charge.

Estaver's argument must have been persuasive, because the Johnsons agreed to drive on to Sentinel. It is unlikely, however, that saving a few dollars on the cost of a hotel room was the catalyst. In the pocket of the rotund contractor was roughly one thousand dollars, a tidy sum of money in 1921.

No one knows what direction the evening would have taken had the Johnsons followed their first inclination and stopped over at the New Cornelia. But they did not do so. What is known is that they made a tragic mistake by allowing themselves to be alone in the desert late at night with Estaver.

Whether by design or accident, Estaver led them onto the wrong road. Instead of heading due west to Sentinel, the lumbering vehicle was pointed southwest toward Stovall. Estaver had assured Johnson that after a few miles the roadway's surface would become hard-packed, but in fact, it was becoming increasingly rutted and more treacherous. Reading his odometer, Johnson announced that they had traveled sixty-one miles since leaving Ajo and "they had gotten no place." It was the wrong thing to have said to Estaver.

Anna Johnson glanced at the odometer and checked her watch. It was about nine-thirty P.M. Disgusted by their lack of progress, she said, "That's what we get for being good and helping out a stranger." They would be the last words spoken by her.

Estaver withdrew a .32 caliber Mauser from the pocket of his Norfolk jacket and, as the aging man turned to speak to him, fired a shot into his neck. "The car stopped," a reporter for the *Arizona Daily Star* would write, "but the engine was still running. When ... [Johnson] reached around to feel and see what was wrong, he was shot a second time, this time in the back."

Bewildered, Anna turned in her seat to see what was happening and was met by a volley of bullets. Two slugs entered her back and a third shattered her brain, causing instant death. Her corpulent body slumped against her husband's, her head fallen into his lap.

Struggling against great pain, Johnson reached around in an effort to grab hold of Estaver. But Estaver was gone. According to later testimony from the wounded man, the assailant had either jumped or fallen from the automobile. Johnson put his foot to the throttle and "got away as fast as he could."

But it was not over yet. As Johnson drove off, Estaver fired two more shots. Both hit their mark. Riddled by four bullets and straining to hang onto consciousness, the Denver tourist proceeded into the blackness of the desert.

Meantime, Estaver, who would later confess to a graceless tumble from the automobile, roamed the desert in search of a glow from the vehicle's tail lamp. Although he had bungled what should have been a simple murder and robbery, he had expended too much effort to allow the obstinate man to drive away and leave him stranded in unfamiliar country.

But Johnson had other ideas. Burdened by the dead weight of Anna's corpse lying against him and ravaged by pain, he summoned his resolve and drove across the desert as far and as fast as he could. Certain that he, too, would die, he was determined to live long enough to report the crime to authorities—to make sure that the nefarious stranger paid for his heinous deed.

He had driven about eight miles when he could drive no more. Bleeding profusely and unable to endure any longer the painful jostling of his wounds, Johnson stopped the car and turned off the engine. Thinking the end was near, he removed some business cards from his vest pocket and scribbled on them that he had been shot and his wife killed by a man they had picked up at the Willard Hotel in Tucson. Upon completion of the task, Johnson lapsed into unconsciousness.

Sun beating against the window glass awakened him the following morning, and the horror of the night reverberated in his mind. Astonished that he was alive, Johnson marshaled his wits as best he could, started the engine of the Dodge touring car, and continued his trek across the desert.

At last, he arrived in the little town of Stovall and stopped the first people he encountered–Walter and Eliza Cronk, tourists from Denver en route to El Paso. After relating details of his ghastly ordeal, he and Cronk located a telephone and attempted to call authorities at Yuma for assistance, but it was impossible to get a connection.

By happenstance, a steam locomotive pulling a passenger train appeared out of the distance, and Cronk went quickly to the track and flagged it down. Aboard the train was J. S. Sullivan, a special officer of the Southern Pacific Railroad police. As Johnson recited his gruesome story, signal maintainer Jack Sleeth happened by. Earlier that morning, Sleeth had come upon a man near the Southern Pacific right-of-way about a mile east of Stovall. The man asked Sleeth where water could be had, then mentioned matter-of-factly that he had been riding with a man and woman who had been held up.

Sleeth and Sullivan set out on a gasoline speedster (the self-propelled cousin of a railroad handcar), certain that the thirsty wanderer was their man. After traveling about two-and-a-half miles, they came upon Estaver walking down the tracks away from Stovall and toward Tucson. Sullivan drew his revolver and ordered the killer to throw up his hands. Estaver prudently complied.

Relieving their prisoner of his .32 caliber Mauser, the railroad men put him aboard the speedster and transported him to Stovall, where Johnson awaited the outcome of their search.

"You scoundrel!" wailed Johnson at the first sight of his wife's murderer. "Why didn't you finish me as you did my wife, so I would be out of my misery?"

Eliza Cronk recounted that Estaver looked Johnson in the eye and replied, "I didn't shoot you last night. Didn't you see two men jump on the running board and shoot you?" It would be the first of countless denials and one that Estaver would take with him to his grave.

According to officer Sullivan, Johnson was weak from loss of blood. A quick examination confirmed that the overweight man had been shot several times. One bullet had entered his neck behind the right ear and emerged from the opposite side. It was miraculous the man was alive and coherent.

Johnson was put aboard the 12:30 P.M. train to Yuma, where he was rushed to the hospital. The next day, the Associated Press would report, "Mr. Johnson's condition still is critical and physicians who are attending him hold out but little hope for his recovery."

Anna's body did not accompany her husband but was "left on the desert" until the following day, when an inquest would be held. It was then taken to Yuma. An autopsy was performed, after which it was given over to a Johnson Undertaking establishment—a coincidence of names not lost on the press.

Estaver was held overnight in Stovall until Sheriff J. M. Polhamus arrived from Yuma to transport the prisoner to the county jail there. Once behind bars, the diminutive shootist loudly proclaimed his innocence, telling anyone who would listen that the Johnsons had been shot by two bandits who leaped out of the brush. He would not be silenced until his court-appointed attorney strongly suggested that Estaver's interests would be better served by shutting his mouth.

An immediate problem facing law officers was to determine in what jurisdiction the shooting had occurred—Yuma, Pima, or Maricopa county. Estaver was returned to the scene of the crime, and after a careful examination of the area, it was concluded that the victims had been gunned down about three miles inside the Pima County line. It was a determination made none too soon.

Incensed by the brutal murder of a hapless woman and the near-fatal shooting of her husband, the citizens of Yuma vowed revenge. Talk of a lynching began as a muted whisper but soon exploded into a deafening cry. When a mob began to form around the jail, Sheriff Polhamus knew he had no choice but to get the prisoner out of Yuma County—fast.

At 9:15 on the evening of November 24, Polhamus secretly removed Estaver from the county jail and whisked him by automobile to Dome, where the heavily shackled prisoner was put aboard a midnight train bound for Tucson.

But word somehow had gotten out, and members of the would-be lynch mob were soon hot on the trail. Masked men scoured the desert flagging down motorists and searching their vehicles for Estaver.

"Innocent or guilty, he was in my safekeeping and I was responsible for him," Polhamus would tell the *Star*. En route to Dome, he had evaded the vigilantes by driving into the Gila River bottom and traveling without headlights. "There was about a foot and one-half of water in the Gila bottom, but we managed to pick out the driest places and were able to navigate without great difficulty, although we could not make much speed."

The following morning, the *Star* would report that "a slender ... man with angular features and a few days growth of beard, arrived in Tucson ... and ate his Thanksgiving dinner in the Pima County jail."

Three days later, Estaver was arraigned before Justice of the Peace Oscar L. Pease, who scheduled a preliminary hearing for December 10. Meantime, Peter Johnson was making a "remarkable" recovery and was expected to be the state's star witness. He disappointed no one.

"Who shot your wife?" inquired Pima County attorney George R. Darnell as the hearing commenced.

"Why, that fellow did it," replied Johnson.

"With trembling finger ... his face twitching with emotion ... [Johnson] pointed to William S. Estaver," reported the *Star*. "Time and time again, the accusing finger was leveled at the defendant, sometimes several words ahead of any direct reference to him."

On December 30, twenty days after the hearing began, Estaver was bound over to superior court to stand trial for first-degree murder. Bail was denied. The *Star* characterized it as "one of the sharpest and most protracted legal battles ever staged in the justice court of the Tucson precinct."

Darnell told reporters that in the absence of any motion by the defense to have the case removed to Tucson, the trial would be held in Ajo during the latter part of January or the first part of February.

None of that came to pass. The trial was tentatively set for March 14 but was moved to April 10, when John L. Van Buskirk, considered one of the state's ablest defense lawyers, entered the case.

Appearing before Superior Court Judge Samuel L. Pattee, who would adjudicate the case, Van Buskirk argued that Johnson and his son, George, had visited Ajo and spoken to everyone in town. Because it was such a small community, the citizens had had an opportunity to discuss the case and form opinions. Pattee recognized the merit of the argument and ordered that the trial be held in Tucson.

In a courtroom packed by curious spectators, opening arguments got under way on March 14 in what would be the lengthiest trial—twelve days—conducted in Pima County since the granting of statehood in 1912.

But regardless of the trial's length, what was perhaps the most damaging testimony against the accused was rendered on the second day by State Senator A. J. Eddy, called by the prosecution as an expert witness in an emerging science that would come to be know as forensics.

"In your opinion, was the bullet found in Mrs. Johnson's body fired from the Estaver gun?"

"Yes."

When the shootings were just three days old, Eddy had begun an exhaustive examination of Estaver's .32 caliber Mauser and the bullets removed from Peter and Anna Johnson's wounds. There was no doubt in his mind that the Mauser was the murder weapon, and he came to court armed with enlarged photographs of bullets he himself had fired from the pistol for comparative purposes.

Deputy County Attorney Ben Matthews asked Eddy, "Do any two guns have the same rifling?"

"No."

Eddy then went into detail about the singular characteristics of firearms and the fact that no two weapons are capable of leaving identical markings on an expended bullet. It was a persuasive argument.

On April 18, the state rested its case. The following day, Estaver took the stand in his own defense. A reporter noted that the accused was "carefully attired in a light brown suit."

Speaking in a voice so low it could scarcely be heard at times, Estaver offered his version of the shooting. "Mrs. Johnson had just been speaking about the harder road that we expected to find near the end of the road to Sentinel. I answered that the road must have changed since I had been over it last, and that I didn't understand why the going was still so rough.

"Just then two shots were fired from the left side of the car. The man was either standing near the car or on the running board, but I think it was on the running board, because as he shot the car stopped and the man took a running step from the car that landed him three feet ahead of the car. Then he darted into the bushes. I took my gun from my hip pocket and fired two shots toward the spot. Mr. Johnson had fallen forward on the [steering] wheel. Suddenly there was one shot or perhaps two fired by a man on the right side, about thirty feet away, and a little ahead of the car. I fired in the direction from which the flash and the explosion had come. As I did so, the car started off again. I lost my balance, fell off the car and landed on my back and shoulders."

Estaver told the court that he was not able to get a good look at the men but was certain they were either Indians or Mexicans. He said that when he fell from the automobile, one of the men dragged him, pushed his face into the sand, and relieved him of his watch and about five hundred dollars in cash.

It was an intriguing tale but could not be substantiated by a single shred of evidence. Nevertheless, some members of the jury apparently found it compelling enough to be influenced by it. On April 22, after deliberating twelve hours, the jury foreman reported to Judge Pattee that he and his cohorts were hopelessly deadlocked.

What the newspapers were fond of calling a "celebrated" trial had ended in a hung jury. The natty little man who told people he was a dentist went back to his cell at the Pima County jail to await the beginning of his second trial, which Pattee had set for May 15.

"Estaver will be tried as many times as necessary to get an acquittal or a conviction, as long as it is possible to obtain juries to try him," declared the county attorney.

As one day passed into another, public interest in the Estaver case ebbed and virtually nothing was written about him in the newspapers. Then on May 6, the *Star* exploded with an astonishing headline: "Estaver Rushed to Florence to Prevent Mob Violence." In the subhead appeared "Killed Texas Sheriff" and "Escaped from Oklahoma Penitentiary."

But perhaps most astonishing was the revelation that Estaver was not Estaver at all. Nor was he Pick, Beck, or Buckmaster. He was not a dentist, either. And he had not come from Detroit. The prim little man partial to Norfolk jackets, stiff collars, puttees, and straw hats was a thirty-six-year-old hardened criminal from Beaumont, Texas, by the name of Paul V. Hadley, who had escaped more than two years before from the penitentiary at McAlester, Oklahoma, where he was serving a life sentence for murder.

Equally astonishing and decidedly disturbing was the fact that Hadley's real identity had positively eluded the Arizona law-enforcement and legal communities.

In 1915 Hadley had been indicted in Jefferson County, Texas, for assault with intent to kill. Rather than face the unpleasantness that might result from a conviction, he fled Texas, thus becoming a fugitive from justice. On March 20, 1916, police in Kansas City, Missouri, arrested a man calling himself J. O. Kendrick, but being possessed of identification skills superior to those of their counterparts in Arizona, they quickly recognized him as the man wanted by Texas authorities.

For reasons unknown, Hadley was locked up in what was called the "matron's section" of the Kansas City Police Department, where his wife, Ida, was allowed to visit him as the couple waited for Jefferson County sheriff Jake Giles to come and claim him.

On March 23, Giles, armed with the necessary papers from Texas, called on the jail to collect his prisoner. There he was met by Ida, who begged him to allow her to accompany her husband on the return trip. Giles told her she could come along if she wanted to but would have to pay her own railroad fare. Ida readily agreed and purchased a ticket to Texas. It would be the costliest decision Giles ever made.

They left Kansas City on the 5:30 P.M. train, Hadley and his wife seated on one side of the aisle, Giles on the other. Having been assured by both husband and wife that the captured fugitive would behave himself, Giles removed Hadley's handcuffs. Another dreadful error.

It was just after midnight, near Muskogee, Oklahoma, when Ida excused herself and slipped into the ladies' room. The sheriff thought nothing of it. About ten minutes later, she returned. As she approached Giles, she removed a pistol from her handbag and blew a hole in the back of his head. The unwitting sheriff died within minutes.

"Don't a man or woman . . . get up," she said menacingly to the passengers as her husband seized the sheriff's gun and rifled papers and money from his pockets.

Next, Ida approached the conductor. "Stop this train or I will blow your brains out." Not one to argue about such a notion, he stopped the train at Checotah, Oklahoma, where the Hadleys disembarked and fled into the darkness.

But it was all for nothing—a brutal, senseless killing. The sheriff of McIntosh County, a man named McCune, got up a posse, and before local residents sat down to lunch, the Hadleys were behind bars.

Each was tried for murder; each was found guilty. Because Ida was deemed mentally unbalanced, she was given an abbreviated sentence of ten years. Hadley was sentenced to life imprisonment.

Then the state of Oklahoma made an amphigoric mistake. Officials agreed to Hadley's request for a sixty-day furlough in order that he might visit his family. The governor's signature was affixed to a piece of paper, and the prisoner walked away from the penitentiary at McAlester never to return. The remainder of his days would be played out in Arizona—violently.

On May 19, 1922, the second trial of Paul V. Hadley, a.k.a. William S. Estaver, opened in Pima County Superior Court. The prosecution's case was substantially the same as developed in the first trial. Hadley's defense, however, was weakened considerably by the new information received from Oklahoma and by sensational publicity attendant to the trial.

Waiting beyond the courtroom door was E. J. Jedlicks, assistant warden of the penitentiary at McAlester. Should the state of Arizona fail to convict Hadley, Jedlicks had a one-way ticket for him to Oklahoma in his pocket.

On May 26, Hadley made the irreversible blunder of taking the stand in his own defense. With his credibility hanging by a thread, he repeated a litany almost identical to that offered at his first trial. But when confronted in cross-examination, he admitted that he was an escaped convict sentenced to life in prison for the murder of a peace officer. It was not an admission that elicited sympathy among the jurors.

"After deliberating for only fifteen minutes," reported the *Star*, "the jury ... returned a verdict ... of first degree murder and recommended that the death penalty be imposed."

It was. Five days later, on June 3, Judge Pattee sentenced Hadley to be "hanged by the neck until dead" on August 18 at the Florence penitentiary. The final chapter of Hadley's checkered life had been written.

Two days before the scheduled execution, the Arizona Supreme Court agreed to hear an appeal, and a stay was granted. No one was surprised. Arguments dragged on through the fall and winter, and on February 6, 1923, the high court upheld both the conviction and the sentence. The execution went back on the docket for Friday, April 13. And this time, the grim reaper would not be denied.

With six days remaining, Hadley's case was taken to the State Board of Pardons in Phoenix, which issued a statement three days later on April 10: "[Hadley] is not deserving of any executive clemency. The evidence adduced abundantly supports the judgment and sentence."

And that was that. Hadley would hang. But not before the *Star* ran a tasteless headline on the front page of its April 12 issue: "What Will Hadley Say Before Rope Put about His Neck?"

He had much to say.

The night before his execution, he borrowed a typewriter from a *Star* reporter and tapped out a statement of some five hundred words proclaiming his innocence and, not surprisingly, lambasting capital punishment.

After suggesting that the death penalty would be stricken from the books if prosecutor, judge and jury were made to carry out executions, Hadley wrote, "While no man wishes to give up his life, death is not a penalty, for if a man is prepared to meet his God, you are just relieving that man of his troubles and placing him in a peaceful rest.

"I believe in God ... and I will not go to His presence with a lie on my lips ... I am not guilty."

The next morning bore witness to yet another gauche headline on the front page of the *Star*. "Hadley meets death without losing nerve—marks last chapter of thrilling murder case."

"Scorning to accept assistance in walking up the flight of stairs from his own cell to the death chamber," chronicled an anonymous *Star* reporter, "Paul Hadley briskly, yet without show of over-confidence, walked directly to the death trap. Halting there he awaited the prison officials as they firmly strapped his arms and legs preparatory to his execution."

The trap was sprung, and Hadley fell through an opening in the floor, dangling eight minutes from a noose before a physician determined that he was dead. Then his body was placed in a "bare wooden box" and interred in the prison cemetery.

The *Tombstone Epitaph*, a journal widely known for its lively prose, carried the least colorful and most sober account of the execution: "[He] mounted the scaffold in the death chamber at the Arizona State Prison shortly before five o'clock this morning, and was hanged for the murder of Mrs. Peter Johnson."

It was Friday the 13th, and it was the first execution ordered by Pima County since statehood. Pick-Beck-Buckmaster-Kendrick-Estaver-Hadley–and whatever else he may have called himself–had committed his last crime.

Bibliography

NEWSPAPERS

Arizona Daily Star (Weekly Star), 29 September 1891 to 8 February 1969

Arizona Daily Sun (Coconino Sun), 28 June to 4 July 1935

The Arizona Republic (Arizona Republican), 20 October 1931 to 2 August 1990

Arizona Silver Belt, 21 April 1930

Bisbee Daily Review, 25 June 1926 to 31 January 1934

Burlingame Advance, 25 July 1934 to 28 September 1944

Chicago Tribune, 22 July 1934 to 28 September 1944

Deseret News (Deseret Evening News), 26 July to 3 September 1953

London Daily Mail, 24 June 1926

Los Angeles Evening Herald Express, 28 October 1937

Los Angeles Examiner, 28 June 1926

Los Angeles Times, 19 May 1926 to 30 September 1944

New York Evening Telegram, 21 February 1930

New York Times, 9 May 1917 to 28 September 1944

Nogales International, 14 September to 23 September 1931

Phoenix Gazette, 30 October 1937

Prescott Evening Courier, 26 July 1953

Sacramento Bee, 4 June 1926

Salt Lake Tribune, 27 July to 4 September 1953

San Diego Herald, 29 July 1926

San Francisco Chronicle, 22 July to 23 July 1934

Tombstone Epitaph, 13 April 1923 to 25 November 1937

Tombstone Nugget, 11 April 1882

Tombstone Prospector, 20 June 1891

Tucson Citizen (Arizona Citizen, Weekly Citizen, Daily Citizen), 6 July 1872 to 5 April 1935

Yuma Morning Star, 21 February 1930

PRESS SERVICES

Associated Press
International News Service
United Press
United Press International

PERIODICALS

Adamic, Louis, "Was Aimee McPherson's Shack in the Grove of Aphrodite?" *Haldeman-Julius Monthly*, October 1926.

Belvin, B. "Sister Aimee." *The New Republic* 9 (1926): 289–91.

Bommersbach, Jana. "The Tilted Scales of Justice." *New Times*, 25 April–1 May 1990.

———. "Wily Winnie." *New Times* 2 May–8 May 1990.

Braly, David. "Oregon Honcho." *True West* 39 (1992): 48–53.

Buehman, Albert R. "Lived Perilously, Died Abruptly." *Arizona Daily Star Album*, 15 (January 1953).

Carr, Harry. "Dillinger's Weaving a Hang-Man's Rope." *Los Angeles Times Sunday Magazine*, 3 June 1934.

Cary, James. "The Untold Story of Short Creek." *American Mercury* 78 (1954): 119–23.

Christiansen, Larry D. "Henceforth and Forever Aimee and Douglas." Parts 1 and 2. *Cochise Quarterly* 8, no. 4 (fall/winter 1978); no. 5 (spring 1979): 5–62.

"Crime." *Time*, 4 June 1934.

Eppinga, Jane. "Good or Bad, Maricopa County Sheriffs Have Never Been Dull." *The Arizona Sheriff* 9, no. 3 (autumn 1990): 23–31.

Fox, Kel M. "Foreman of the Jury: Sidelights on the Trial of Winnie Ruth Judd." *The Journal of Arizona History* 26, no. 3 (autumn 1985): 295–306.

"The Government's Effective War Against Crime." *The Literary Digest*, 8 December 1934.

Hamilton, William B. "American Characters." *American Heritage*, October 1977.

"Hide Behind the Law." *Star Detective Magazine*, (Date unknown), 41–43, 68–91.

Jeffrey, John Mason. "Discipline in the Arizona Territorial Prison: Draconian Severity of Enlightened Administration?" *The Journal of Arizona History* 9, no. 3 (autumn 1968): 140–154.

Leavengood, Betty. "Cheap Shots, Morphine Shots and Gun Shots." *Tucson Magazine*, November–December 1989.

Lefler, Jack. "Winnie Ruth Judd: Famous Crimes No. 2." *Arizona Daily Star Roundup*, (23 May 1954): 6.

Maloney, Wiley S. "Short Creek Story." *American West* 11, no. 2 (March 1974): 16–23, 60–62.

Roberts, Virginia Cullen. "Mary Page Handy and the Lawyer Who Dared to Defend Her." *The Journal of Arizona History* 30, no. 4 (winter 1989): 365–390.

Ryder, David Warren. "Aimee Semple McPherson." *The Nation* 123 (July 28, 1926) 81–82.

Sinclair, Upton. "The Evangelist Drowns." *The New Republic* 47 (June 30, 1926): 171.

Smith, Dean. "In Cold Blood." *Arizona Trend* (August 1988): 69–71.

Steele, Henry Joseph. "Bernhardt of the Sawdust Trail." *Vanity Fair* 40, no. 1 (March 1933): 38–41.

Stocker, Joseph. "Incident at Short Creek." *Frontier* (September 1953).

Woodcock, Michael L. "…Hanged by the Neck Until Dead." *Arizona History Magazine* 5, no. 6 (November–December 1988): 3.

BOOKS

Barnes, Will C. *Arizona Place Names.*
Tucson: University of Arizona Press, 1936.

Beverly, Nichols. "Christ in Vaudville," in
The Star Spangled Manner. New York:
Doubleday, 1930.

Bond, Ervin. *Percy Bowden: Born to be a
Frontier Lawman.* Douglas, Arizona, 1976.
N.p., n.d.

Brent, William and Milarde Brent. *The
Hell Hole.* Yuma, Arizona, 1962. N.p., n.d.

Crow, Rosalie, and Sidney B. Brinckerhoff.
Early Yuma. Flagstaff, Arizona: Northland
Press, 1976.

Ericksen, Ephraim Edward. *The
Psychological and Ethical Aspects of
Mormon Group Life.* Chicago: University
of Chicago Press, 1922.

Goben, John D., Rev. *Aimee the Gospel
Gold Digger.* Los Angeles: Peoples
Publishing Co., 1932.

Jeffrey, John Mason. *Adobe and Iron.*
La Jolla, California: Prospect Avenue Press,
1969.

Jennings, Renz L. *The Boy from Taylor.*
Phoenix, Arizona, 1977. N.p., n.d.

Love, Frank. *From Brothel to Boomtown.*
Colorado Springs: Little London Press,
1981.

Malmquist, O. N. *The First 100 Years: A
History of the Salt Lake Tribune 1871–1971.*
Salt Lake City: Utah State Historical
Society, 1971.

Mavity, Nancy Barr. *Sister Aimee.* Garden
City: Doubleday, Doran and Co., 1931.

McClintock, James H. *Mormon Settlement
in Arizona.* Phoenix: State of Arizona, 1921.

McPherson, Aimee Semple. *The Story of
My Life.* Hollywood: International
Correspondents Publication, 1951.

Myrick, David F. *Railroads of Arizona.* 3
vols. Berkeley: Howell-North Books, 1975.

Rider, Rowland W. *The Roll Away Saloon.*
Logan: Utah State University Press, 1985.

Sonnichsen, C. L. *Tucson.* Norman:
University of Oklahoma Press, 1982.

Spicer, Edward M., and Raymond H.
Thompson, eds. *Plural Society in the
Southwest.* New York: The Weatherhead
Foundation, 1972.

Thompson, Vicki. *Across the Dry Rillito.*
Tucson: Territorial Publishers, Inc., 1968.

Trafzer, Cliff, and Steve George. *Prison
Centennial, 1876–1976.* Yuma, Arizona: Rio
Colorado Press, 1980.

Index

AFTER A CAREER OF more than twenty years as an interviewer, news director, and producer, W. Lane Rogers left broadcasting in 1987 to become a full-time writer and historian. He has published more than 400 articles in worldwide publications including the *Journal of Arizona History* and is currently book review editor of the *Tombstone Epitaph*, a monthly journal of western history with subscribers in all fifty states as well as twenty-eight foreign countries. His "From Colonia Dublán to Binghampton: The Mormon Odyssey of Frederick, Nancy, and Amanda Williams" received the Arizona Historical Society's C. L. Sonnichsen award for best article in 1994. *Crimes and Misdeeds*, Rogers' first published book, is the result of accidental findings—headlines he came across in old newspapers while doing other research.

Rogers and his wife live in a turn-of-the-century adobe house in one of Tucson's historic districts, and share their home with five dogs and four cats.